DISCOVER HEALING FROM TRAGEDY
REVEAL RESILIENCE
AND LEAVE A LASTING LEGACY

*Your*
# STORY
*Your*
# STRENGTH

## KELLY SNIDER

PUBLISHED BY EPIC EXCHANGES MEDIA

Published by Epic Exchanges Media, November 2022
ISBN: 978-1-7775552-2-1

Editor: Danielle Anderson
Proofreader: April Lemoine
Cover Design & Typeset: Tara Eymundson
Cover Art: "Anka" by Emily Scott

# Dedication

To the grandparents, parents, and parental figures who
poured their time, love, and affection into teaching me
through their own words and stories, but mostly through
their actions and examples. I love and miss you all.

# Contents

# Introduction

One day, in the early morning hours, I was awoken from deep sleep by heavy coughing. My eyes started stinging, and I cried out in pain to my parents. When no response came, my crying turned to screaming.

This was the day my life changed forever, and where my journey to discovering the incredible power of my story—of all our stories—began.

I don't have any advanced degrees in medicine, neurology, social work, psychology, or counselling to inform what I'll be sharing with you in this book. What I do have is fifty years of lived experience working to understand how my journey has shaped who I am today and to learn how to heal the wounds that many of us encounter throughout our lives. I've read the books, I've taken the courses, I've seen the therapists, and I've had innumerable conversations looking for that knowledge, that understanding, that "a-ha" moment of clarity that would "fix" everything I have deemed wrong with me.

But there's no magic pill or quick fix, because our stories, our patterns, weren't built in an instant. We have to do the work to discover the unique path our stories have set us upon.

I know what you're thinking: "Not another person telling me that story is the key to everything!"

Yes, "story"—or rather, telling our stories—has become something of a trend these days. You see and hear about it in the news, in advertising, in marketing, in the business world, even across every social media platform.

That's because it works. We connect with stories in a way that we don't connect with facts and statistics. Stories include emotion, and when that emotion is conveyed well, we feel it. And when we feel emotion, we are more likely to engage with whatever is telling that story. For example, if we see a product making someone else feel more successful, smarter, stronger, whatever it is that we might want in our own lives, we are more likely to purchase that product.

Even before there was written language, early societies told stories using images like the drawings that were found inside caves. They also used storytelling to pass on knowledge to younger generations. That early storytelling was necessary for our very survival; it's how we learned that a plant was poisonous or that an animal was dangerous.

Stories are also an important part of learning to make sense of our world, and as civilizations grew, they have helped each successive generation build on our experience and knowledge because we don't have to learn that same piece of information over and over again. We can take what we've already learned and add to that knowledge through our own experiences.

Stories make us root for the underdog or help us love or hate the celebrity of the day. They're what make us emotional when we watch an athlete win an Olympic medal or step away from their race to help someone else on the Special Olympics track. They help us connect with others, define our own aspirations, and persevere when the going gets tough. Because if someone else has accomplished it, then it's possible for me to do it as well.

So yes, stories sell.

This book isn't about all of that, though the stories you discover here could also be used for marketing purposes. This book is about diving into our own stories and those of the people who have influenced who we are, what we believe about ourselves, and how we interact with everything around us so that we can understand how we developed our hopes and dreams and the way we view our role in this world.

By understanding our stories—the blessings and the burdens, the triumphs and the traumas, the victories and the vanquishments—we find our strength. We find what we are truly made of and all that we bring to this world.

Our stories are the key to connecting with our past, present, and future. Through our stories, we recognize that while life is never perfect, everything we experience teaches us something new—something that we can embrace, integrate into our lives, and then pass on to others. We can make a difference: in our own lives, in the lives of those we care about, and even, if we choose to do so, in the world that we live in.

It was Mahatma Gandhi who said, "Be the change you wish to see in the world." In order to BE that change, we need to truly understand, accept, and embrace who we truly are. And our experiences—our stories—help us do just that.

# The Beginning

❋

*"We keep moving forward, opening new doors,
and doing new things, because we're curious and
curiosity keeps leading us down new paths."*
— *Walt Disney*

# Where It Starts

*What the hell was I thinking?*

That was the thought overwhelming me as I made my way to a spa retreat where I would spend the next six weeks away from my family, friends, and life. As a few tears squeezed out of my eyes and ran down my cheeks, I questioned if I was doing the right thing.

This getaway, which I had been planning for the past four months, was in no way a hardship. I wasn't going to be without people. I wasn't going to be without internet or cell service or any other way to stay in touch with my family or friends. I wasn't going to be roughing it by any stretch of the imagination.

And yet these coming weeks would bring about so much change. I was literally picking myself up out of my daily routine and stripping away all the demands on my time and energy—all the demands that came from work, from commitments, from friends, from family, and from my expectations of myself in all those relationships.

And I was terrified.

⋇

Nine months before this van ride, life was somewhat predictable—normal, you could say. I was renting a great suite with fun neighbours in a fourplex building that was close enough to all my family that we could stay connected and involved. I was ten years into my event producing career, specializing in large gala-style events for all kinds of charities. I'd partnered with health charities, theatre and dance companies, even churches and camps. My typical day was filled with anything from administrative tasks to meetings with volunteers, suppliers, sponsors or event hosts to ensure a successful event.

On this particular day I was sitting in a restaurant, waiting for a local news anchor to join me for lunch with the plan to ask her to be the honorary chair for a holiday event. Then my cell phone rang—a good reminder to turn it off before my guest arrived. I pulled it out and noticed it was my mother calling. She *never* called in the middle of the day. So, I answered.

Time stopped as she told me that my thirty-eight-year-old sister-in-law had suffered a massive stroke that morning and was currently in the ICU.

It's not my place to tell my sister-in-law's story—or anyone else's story, for that matter. I can, however, talk about the way I responded to this event and the impact it had on me. Because when things like this happen, when families experience trauma and tragedy, the rest of life doesn't just stop so we can take care of our loved ones.

In the months that followed, I did what I have always done: I tried to fix things in whatever way I could. For me, that meant being available to help at any time. If my brother or one of his boys or anyone else in my family needed something, I always tried to be there for them. And in the midst of this upheaval, my regular life continued. I purchased my first home, planned some minor renovations (which turned out to be not so minor), and moved. In addition, I was planning events for multiple clients, working more than full time if I were to add up all the hours.

As you might imagine, my life became overwhelming. And with that, I began to unravel.

I'd always felt my role was to take care of everyone else—not just my family, but my colleagues, volunteers, friends, anyone and everyone I cared about. As a result, I had stopped taking care of myself, if I had ever really taken care of myself at all. I never wanted to be the one that needed help. I never wanted to be that squeaky wheel that needed attention, even my own. I rarely stopped to even *think* about taking care of myself. I was stuck on that hamster wheel of never-ending activity, and I felt guilty if I even thought about taking a break. There were always things that needed doing, people that needed help, work deadlines approaching. Who would take care of them if it wasn't me?

And then one day, I lost it. I fell apart. My carefully controlled emotions broke loose when I was with a group of friends. I found myself yelling, cursing, crying, and telling everyone that there was no way they could understand how much I was carrying between the pressures of family, volunteer commitments, work, and being a new homeowner. Not to mention that I was also still being affected by all my old trauma, which had been triggered anew by my sister-in-law's stroke and ensuing complications. It was a *lot*.

That's when I realized that I had been burning the proverbial candle not only at both ends but also right through the middle. I was likely extremely close to ending up in the hospital, not with an injury but with a complete breakdown. I needed to change something.

Or everything.

I'd heard or read somewhere that it takes three weeks to break a bad habit and another three weeks to create a new, better one. Which meant, of course, that I needed six weeks to fix everything that was wrong with me. (And yes, I'm being sarcastic.)

So, I did my research and found a place I could go for an extended stay. A place where I could focus on myself in all areas: physical, emotional, mental, and spiritual. Which is how I found myself in the back of that van, questioning everything.

And that's when I was faced with the stark reality of my life.

Besides the fact that it was the first time I was really travelling on my own—I didn't know anybody at my destination and the resort was in a city and state I'd never been to before—I was also going to have to face the difficult truth of just how unhealthy I had allowed myself to become. However, somewhere deep down I must have known that this fear and discomfort wasn't just about being alone. It also wasn't just about eating better and exercising. It was about facing the truth that my life was about to change. That my life *needed* to change.

Looking back now, I don't think I was fully aware of just how unhealthy I was at that time. Or perhaps I was aware on some level, but I wasn't fully acknowledging just how bad it had gotten. And the reality was pretty grim.

Physically, I was heading down a very scary road. My diet sucked. Too often I would grab whatever was easiest to give me a hit of energy: a caffeinated beverage, a sandwich, or something sweet, usually eaten in my car or at my desk. When I was home, I'd grab a bowl of cereal, some popcorn, or a takeout meal. I had a gym membership—or two—but I couldn't remember the last time I had really exercised, let alone made it a regular part of my week. I was overweight (and had been for most of my teenage and adult life) and pre-diabetic, with high blood sugar and high blood pressure and medications for both.

Mentally and emotionally, I was exhausted and burned out, and that was before I knew burn out was a thing. I'd seen a few different therapists and counsellors over the years but never really gotten anywhere because I wouldn't let what I considered to be the more difficult emotions surface. I didn't want to go there. In fact, I had spent most years pushing those emotions down and away. My mind never turned off because I kept it busy—even if I was home alone, the radio or television was on in the background, often turned to a news channel.

Spiritually, I was great at pretending I had it all together. I attended church and home group (a small group of friends who met weekly to discuss sermon topics and support one another) and even held roles of responsibility within the church I attended in addition to being part of the worship team. From the outside, it looked like life was good—that I was doing well—but that was because I was playing a role more than I was feeling truly connected to my faith. It all kept my calendar full, but most of the time I was going through the motions and portraying what I thought people wanted to see.

These six weeks were an opportunity to change it all. An opportunity to be in an environment that was all about supporting a healthy lifestyle, from food and activity to rest and rejuvenation. An opportunity to dive into the mindset and psychology that had kept me in these unhealthy cycles. It was even an opportunity to explore my spiritual life and reconnect with what I believed and why I believed it.

Once I arrived at the resort, I got my room, unpacked, and dove right in. Because that's what you do when you want to make some huge life changes, right?

Actually, that's not what I did. I was too tired. Bone-deep tired. Yes, I unpacked. Then I went to dinner, where I sat by myself and reviewed my plans for the week.

And then, for much of the next few days, I slept.

Even when I was planning this trip, that exhausted part of me knew that I would need some time to settle in. So, I hadn't scheduled much for those first days. I went to breakfast if I woke up on time. I walked in the warm desert sunshine. I went to lunch. I slept. I read a novel or two, maybe even three. I had dinner. And then I slept some more.

Somewhere around the morning of day four, as I was walking to the dining room for breakfast, I had the thought, *It's all about me.* For the first time that I could remember, I wasn't rushing to fulfill someone else's needs. I wasn't putting aside something I wanted to be present for someone else. I wasn't filling my day with meetings, tasks, and appointments based on what someone else wanted or expected from me, or even what I *thought* someone else wanted or needed from me.

It was all about me. What I wanted or didn't want. What I *needed*.

In that very moment, life started to change. I didn't know it yet, but I was about to receive some crucial lessons on the importance of embracing and sharing your story. And it was only once I let go of everyone's expectations and focused on myself that I was able to learn this lesson.

Since this retreat, I have realized that the stories that make up who we are remind us of the things that are important, the things that light us up, the lessons we have learned, and the gifts that our experiences have brought to our lives and to the lives of others. And when we know who we are and what is important, we can be more authentic and share more of our true selves with others.

Our stories have power, yours included. And *you* are the only one who can tell your story.

# Imposter Syndrome

B ack in those early days of my six-week retreat, I kept to myself most of the time. However, once I had the realization that it was all about me, I relaxed a little and started reaching out to others. At breakfast, I asked the person at the table next to mine about her smoothie, which I hadn't seen on the menu. I chatted with the staff member who was keeping an eye on everyone using the cardio machines in the gym. I even asked to sit at the captain's table—a spot where those who were travelling on their own could share a meal with others. Lunches were generally hosted by a staff member, a different one each day, who would highlight one of the programs offered by the resort. One day it might be an exercise physiologist, the next a nutritionist or a doctor. There was even an astrologer and a clairvoyant. I met some fascinating people during the meals at these communal tables: a stand-up comic, a television director, a sports commentator, college students, entrepreneurs, businesspeople from all sectors. I even developed some friendships that still exist today, more than fifteen years later.

Pretty much every conversation at the captain's table started out with people asking where you were from and how long you were staying. My response of six weeks stood out and had people asking why—most people stayed for a few days, maybe a week at most. My standard answer was that I decided I needed three weeks to break my bad habits and three weeks to replace them with good ones so I could be healthier in every way. Most of the time, that was enough and the person moved on. Occasionally my response led to more questions, more conversation. But even then, I rarely got into the details of everything that brought me there. After all, who knew when I would see these people again after they left? Or even after this meal?

Then one day, I bumped into the staff member who had been at the lunch table with us a few days prior. She was so excited to see me. She said that she had just said goodbye to a couple who had been at the table, and they couldn't stop talking about me and how inspired they were by my decision to take six weeks out of my regular life to take care of my own health.

I remember thinking that was crazy. Who was I to inspire anyone else? In fact, I'd done everything wrong. I was overweight, unhealthy, and burned out. I was a fraud in so many ways. I did not have it all together. If they only knew just how much of a *mess* I really was!

Maybe you've had similar thoughts about your experiences, your story, or even yourself. Maybe you've asked yourself questions like: Who would really care about me or my story? Who would ever give me an award? I don't really deserve that job, that promotion, that raise. Who am I to… you can fill in the rest.

Well, you are not alone. Truth be told, I feel it in every single thing I do. Who am I to write a book? Who am I to have a podcast? Who am I to put myself out there as an expert in any area, or even as someone who is knowledgeable about anything?

And it's not just the two of us either. According to the American Psychological Association, an estimated seventy percent of people—women and men—experience these types of feelings at some point in their lives. This includes Academy-Award-winning actors, Grammy-winning musicians, Olympic gold medalists, CEOs, entrepreneurs, grandparents, moms, dads, students, people from all walks of life with all kinds of accolades and backgrounds. No one is immune.

If you've ever been plagued with feelings of self-doubt or insecurity, then you are familiar with that voice inside your head that says you don't know what you're doing, you shouldn't be there, and someone will find out that you've been faking it all along. *Many* successful people experience these thoughts and feelings, and they don't let it stop them from accomplishing great things.

Quite often, getting past these doubts starts with understanding our stories. Our stories can help us recognize where some of these thoughts may have started, such as feeling like your grades were never good enough to meet your parents' expectations or like you couldn't live up to the accomplishments of your siblings. Perhaps it was the existence of basic stereotypes, like "women are weaker than men at math and science" or "successful people dress and act a certain way." It could even be how you feel about or relate to money, success, or wealth, including thoughts like "rich people are selfish and shallow" or "money is the root of all evil."

When we revisit these stories from our formative years, we receive a greater understanding of where some of those thoughts and beliefs may have started. And when we recognize those origins, we can start to dismantle these belief systems using the truth from our experiences, our accomplishments, and even our mistakes—after all, every mistake brings us one step closer to getting it right the next time.

In order to find the value in our stories, we must stop comparing ourselves to everyone else and focus on our own progress. We are not the same naïve person looking for our first job, or the same innocent teen entering into our first relationship, or the same brand-new parent unsure of how to care for a newborn. We have to stop downplaying how much we have accomplished and how far we have come. Everything we've gone through has taken us a step further in our journey. The people we look to for inspiration, advice, or mentorship are often many steps ahead of us and on a completely different path than our own. It's time to stop comparing and start recognizing our own strengths, accomplishments, growth, successes, and value. And our stories are the key to achieving this.

# Not a Victim

One of the reasons we are so reluctant to talk about ourselves, especially what we have achieved or overcome, is that there are so many different definitions of success. And when it comes to major life achievements, the line keeps moving. Take education or business or even personal growth as an example. Simply starting or completing a stage like high school or university or a landing a new job is an achievement in and of itself. Heck, even changing your mindset is an accomplishment worth celebrating. However, more often than not we are constantly looking ahead to the next step, the next degree, the next level. When we do this, we can never win, because that finish line keeps moving.

The negative events in our lives can make this whole situation even more complicated. If we have experienced difficult times—trauma, tragedy, major losses, those big challenges we face in life—we can get stuck in the emotion of that incident. Often, that makes us feel as though our worlds are unravelling. The tendency is to then retreat into ourselves and put on a mask that projects an image of having it all together. However, the longer we keep this mask up, the more we worry about what others might think of us should they discover the truth. We worry that sharing what is really going on opens us up to judgment or pity—or worse, to being seen as a victim.

Sometimes when we think about sharing our story, we worry about playing the victim. Because let's face it, we all have known or met someone who comes across as wanting attention or playing the victim, and we don't want to be *that* person. We fear that talking about our story might put us in that space, resulting in others pitying us or thinking of us as weak.

I've struggled with this as well.

Consider the word orphan. What comes to mind when you see or hear that word? Likely images of Oliver Twist saying, "Please sir, may I have some more?" or Annie with her "Hard Knock Life." Or perhaps you picture Oliver learning to survive on the streets under the tutelage of the thief Fagin, or Annie making friends with the monkey that climbs across the rooftop and into her attic bedroom, or even the rags-to-riches endings where Oliver finds his family and an inheritance and Annie is adopted by Daddy Warbucks.

Does your image of the word "orphan" still fit as a description for Oliver and Annie at the finale of their stories? Or does it feel wrong, perhaps uncomfortable and too sad for their fairy-tale endings?

What if I mentioned people like Edgar Allen Poe, Eleanor Roosevelt, Babe Ruth, Marilyn Monroe, John Lennon, Steve Jobs, even Jamie Foxx? Would your feelings about any of them change if you knew they were orphaned either by death or abandonment? Would you feel they deserved their success any more or less? Would it prompt you to be more forgiving of any bad behaviour? Would it lessen any envy or jealousy you have of their achievements?

I am also an orphan. Maybe you already knew that about me, but you are quite possibly learning this for the first time. Did it change the way you feel about me? Do you now value my story any more or less? Did some pitying thoughts come up? Did that label make you think of me as a victim?

All of those questions are the reason why, for most of my life, I

*15*

was hesitant to tell people my whole story. I didn't want to be pitied, and I definitely didn't want to be seen as a victim. However, I hit a point several years ago where I had to tell my story in order to get the answers I needed, and doing so was an incredible experience.

When I was just three years old, my parents fell asleep while smoking. A cigarette fell between the cushions in their bedroom and started a very smoky fire. A gentleman was driving his daughter to her summer job when he saw smoke billowing around our house, so he stopped to see if anyone needed help. When he did, heard a child screaming. With no thought for his own safety, he broke into the house and battled the thick smoke. It took him three attempts before he was able to reach me and bring me out safely. He tried one more time to get to my baby sister, but the smoke was too much for him—thankfully, the firemen arrived in time to get her out as well. Sadly, our parents did not survive.

Over thirty years later, my grandfather passed away. As I was going through his belongings, I found a file filled with newspaper clippings about the tragic event, including a story on the man who saved my sister and me. The article featured a photo of him and his daughter, who would have been about seventeen years old at the time.

Through the articles, I learned that he had taught in a neighbouring school district, so I asked my teacher friends if they knew him or knew of him. But of course, with so much time having passed, nobody I spoke with knew who he was. Every year or two, I would try another way to find him without any luck.

A few years later, I joined a Facebook group for people who had grown up in my city. There were often informative and interesting conversations going on about the history of the area, and about many of the people who grew up there. I noticed that many people would use this page to connect with long-lost friends from their school days and realized that posting here could possibly help me find this man or his daughter, because either they had lived nearby or she had worked in the area.

It took me a few days to talk myself into posting the articles and asking my questions. Why? Because I was nervous about putting my story out there. I didn't want anyone to pity me or see me as a victim, nor did I want to draw attention to myself or my story. However, none of the other ways I'd attempted to find this man had worked.

So, I decided to take the plunge and make this piece of my story public.

I scanned and posted the newspaper articles and asked, "Does anyone know or remember the father and daughter in these stories and articles?" And then I held my breath and waited for a response, any response—though not nearly as long as I thought I might.

Not even two minutes later, the first response came: "That's me. Are you the little girl?" It was the man's daughter! I was stunned. And shocked. And even a little overwhelmed.

"Yes, I am," I responded.

This led to a short exchange over private message where I found out that my grandfather had kept in touch with her father for a short time, that she and her dad often wondered about my sister and me, and that he would have been so happy to know we stayed together after the fire. Sadly, he passed away in 2001 so I never was able to connect with him personally.

But this exchange with his daughter wasn't all that came from sharing this small part of my story. Throughout the morning, more people joined in on the conversation: people who remembered the event, former neighbours who remembered my parents fondly, people who had lived in the same place before and after us and recognized the house, firefighters who had attended the scene—one who even quit the job after this event because it hit too close to home. I even heard from the police officer who had the unenviable task of notifying my grandparents.

When I first decided to post the articles, I had hoped to find someone who had gone to school with the daughter or perhaps worked with her. I never expected to find her so quickly, and I certainly never believed there would be such a flood of responses.

My story connected people. It filled in more information, not only for me but also for many others who played a role, however small, in that piece of my story. And just posting the information inspired others to share their own memories of that day and of my parents—to reflect on what it had meant in their own lives and to connect with people from their past.

I also had friends reach out to me who were following the posts throughout the day. Some of them knew my history, but for others it came as a surprise. Many reached out to share their thoughts and emotions with me. Not one of these people felt pity for me, nor did they see me as a victim. Instead, they remarked on the strength, resiliency, and courage they took from the entire thread of messages.

When these big life-changing events happen, we can often get caught up in wrestling with the questions of "why me?" or "why now?" as we search for value, purpose, and meaning in these experiences. The only way to find that meaning and purpose is to take the time to dig into your story—ALL of your story.

When we take the time to sit with our stories, to journal about them, to talk about them with someone we trust, we realize that other people do not see us as the victim, nor do they pity us. They see and know who we are now and how far we've come.

And once we have this realization, the way we view ourselves changes. We don't feel like the victim anymore; we can see the bigger picture, and we can acknowledge our growth.

Our stories don't have to define us or put a label on us. Instead, they lay the framework for the transformations we've experienced— and for those still to come. We can take these labels and say, this is who I was, how I related to the world at one time, but no longer. I learned something from this experience about who I no longer wanted to be—and even more so, I learned who I wanted to become.

By shifting our perspective in this way, our challenging or difficult experiences go from a story to be pitied into a story that will inspire that same change in someone else. We can cast away the label of "victim" and embrace the power of sharing our experiences with the world.

# The Healing Power of Story

Each of us is the hero of our own constantly-unfolding tale—one that no one else can write. However, too many of us leave these stories untold. Why? Many reasons, but perhaps mostly because we feel unworthy or unimportant or even boring when we compare our own stories with those we see and hear in the media.

However, when we deny ourselves the opportunity of sharing, we can actually *create* illness. It starts with those feelings of unworthiness, unimportance, loneliness, and likely many more emotions that we don't want to acknowledge. We put on a mask each day that covers them up and falsely tells the world that we have it all together. All the while, we are feeling a vague sense that something isn't quite right—that we are out of alignment, perhaps even feeling out of touch with our life's purpose.

Our bodies react to these feelings and start releasing hormones like cortisol and epinephrine—stress hormones that are triggered by depression, anxiety, fear, anger, and more. These hormones create inflammation, which turns your body into breeding ground for illness. This creates more stress, which releases more of these hormones, and so on and so on—a never-ending cycle.

When we're stuck in this loop, it's easy to feel isolated and disconnected from the people around us—particularly when we compare what we are experiencing to the carefully curated lives we see on social media. It's not often that the question "how are you?" is answered with anything but "fine," "good," or even more often these days, "busy." This leaves us feeling like we are the only one who doesn't have it all together, the only one who is struggling, and that isolation grows. And that's exactly how I felt at so many times throughout my life:

- At seven, when I was trying to grasp my identity after being adopted and having to deny the first last name I'd ever known;

- At twelve, when I would escape into a world of books where everything was solved by the final page;

- At eighteen, when I was caught between who I was discovering myself to be and who others seemed to expect me to be;

- At nineteen, when a three-year-old's tantrum over wanting his mommy triggered my own long-suppressed grief over losing my parents at the same age (we'll get back to this later);

- At twenty-six, when I was suddenly overcome by anxiety and panic attacks as I discovered early life sexual abuse that my mind and memory had repressed for almost twenty years;

- At thirty-six, after my sister-in-law's stroke and my ensuing need to be the fixer left me depleted and unable to make even the simplest of decisions;

- And much of my life while dealing with food issues and disordered eating patterns that I hid from family and friends.

I've already talked about how sharing what I considered to be small pieces of my story led me to the realization that others could be inspired or encouraged by our stories. What I haven't touched on yet is the healing journey that this realization set me upon.

You see, the more I dove into trying to understand these events in my life and the emotions that came with them, the more I understood that all stories (both our own and those of the important people in our lives) have a lasting impact on us. But even when I was journaling all of this, I still felt isolated and alone in it all.

What also started happening is something I wasn't even aware of at the time. The more I understood about *myself* in the midst of all these difficult events, the more I just naturally started to share with the people close to me—the ones I felt safe with. Unintentionally. I even had a good friend tell me after a two-hour lunch that she felt she learned more about me in that conversation than she had in the previous ten years of knowing me!

And that is part of the key here: to really ignite this healing process, we need to have our stories witnessed by people who care. People who won't sit in judgment. People who don't have expectations of who you are or who they want you to be. People who will—and do—accept you as you are, whether you've got it all together or not!

And when we do this—when we lay our struggles and failures and disappointments and emotions out—we allow others to show us that we're not alone in our experiences.

This is where we find connection.

Consider the #MeToo movement. The phrase #MeToo was created in 2006 by social activist Tarana Burke as part of a grassroots campaign focused on women of colour who had experienced sexual abuse. In 2017, actress Alyssa Milano popularized it by calling for all women who had been sexually harassed or assaulted to write #MeToo on their social media posts in order to show the magnitude of the problem. Subsequent polls showed that more than 50% of North American women reported receiving unwanted and inappropriate sexual advances, and over one third of women *worldwide* are estimated to be affected by sexual violence. These are staggering statistics.

But here's the thing: when women started using the hashtag, it brought friends, families, and communities together. All these people who had previously been quiet about their experiences, perhaps due to shame or powerlessness or not wanting to "rock the boat," discovered that there were so many others who understood, who had been through similar situations, and who supported them and their experiences. A community sprung up around these women—a community of listeners, supporters, and fighters—and they realized they *did* have a voice. They found others who were just like them, they found strength in numbers, and they have since created—and are still creating—change.

That's exactly what happens when we share part of our own story. We find validation. We find community. We find support. And that builds even more strength, community, and ultimately, resilience.

But the ultimate power that comes with telling and sharing your story is the infinitely positive effect it has on your inner self. It lowers your levels of cortisol and epinephrine (those stress hormones we talked about). And even better than that, it signals your body to start releasing the "good" hormones like oxytocin, dopamine, and endorphins. These hormones not only make you feel good, but also trigger your body's self-repair mechanisms—kind of like a dose of preventative medicine.

As you can see, sharing our stories can be healing in many ways—but only if the sharing is done in the right way. Before we step up and tell our story, we need to be able to do so from a positive place, one where we've found the good in the challenge or struggle. We have to take steps to heal our story before our story can heal us.

# Healing

*

*"Storms make trees take deeper roots."*

— *Dolly Parton*

# We Are All Broken

'm not the only person who has dealt with tragedy or trauma. In fact, it's incredibly likely that most of the people you interact with have overcome some big, emotional, life-changing challenges. Maybe you've experienced some of these challenges yourself. And it's through these difficulties and experiences that we learn something about ourselves, generally coming out of them stronger, wiser, and better than before.

A few years ago, I worked with some former classmates to plan our thirtieth high school reunion. We'd already had a couple by this point, and while it was always fun to see people and reminisce, it always felt a little like there was this subtle layer of competition. Who looked the best? Who had married well? Who had the most success in their career? Who showed up in the most expensive or exotic car? Who had kids, and how smart or accomplished were they? I even remember a former classmate asking me at our ten-year reunion if anyone was famous yet.

Because of all this, I never really looked forward to attending these events. In the days leading up to this reunion, I was feeling a little anxious about the posturing I was expecting to happen. However, this reunion was different—more relaxed and fun than any of the previous ones had been. People were having real conversations and connecting with others in ways they never had before. They were sharing struggles. Sharing loss. Sharing life.

And I wasn't the only one that felt this way. In several conversations I had following the event, people commented on the fact that it felt better. That they connected more. That they walked away with more positive feelings than they had ever expected.

What made this reunion so different? I believe that it was because people started to realize that at some point, we all experience struggles and difficulties and yes, even trauma and tragedy. Whatever that looks like in each of our lives, the result is the same: we discover that we are all broken in some way. Maybe it's the death of a parent, friend, spouse, or child. Maybe it's an accident or illness or divorce. Maybe it's rape or abuse or letting go and mourning a long-held dream. Quite likely, it's a combination of several such events.

The connecting piece is that we had all walked through difficult times, and we'd come out the other side a different person. Wiser. Stronger. Scarred. And one day, we realized that everyone has been through something, whether we knew it or not. So, we became more accepting. Instead of trying to put people into a box or label them, we started taking the time to find out what's under the surface.

Everyone in this world is broken in some way, but broken doesn't have to mean flawed. The Japanese art of kintsugi teaches us that broken objects are not something to hide but to instead be displayed with pride. It involves using a precious metal—gold, silver, or lacquer dusted with powdered gold—to bring together the broken pieces while enhancing the breaks at the same time, adding value to a piece that we might otherwise throw away and replace. The repair takes time, up to a month, as there are many different steps with drying and setting times required throughout the process. But in the end, every repaired piece is stronger, more beautiful, and more precious than the original. And no two pieces are ever the same because each object will break in a different way.

And so it is with us. When we break—when we have these difficult life experiences—we do so in ways that are unique to who we are and to our particular situation. Some of us may take longer to heal than others, but ultimately, we are all changed by these experiences. They make us stronger, more beautiful, and more precious in our own unique way.

When we experience these times that break us, it levels the playing field, so to speak. When we see how easily we can hide our pain and struggle from others, we realize that every single person we meet has, is, or will be fighting some kind of battle, some kind of brokenness, that we cannot see. And when we've gone through these challenges ourselves, we are more able to recognize that broken (and beautiful) place in others.

To bring it all back to my most recent high school reunion, the fact that all of us had been broken by something over the years allowed us to see the unique beauty and preciousness in the people around us. As a result, we were able to be more authentic and real rather than pretending everything was great in order to live up to some projected expectation (which, let's be honest, we usually set for ourselves). And that made for a more fun, more inclusive, and more honest gathering. Connections were reborn—and, in some cases, brand new ones were formed. Wounds were healed as apologies were made for damage done by thoughtless words and actions during those teenage years. We were able to move past the superficial and accept each other on a deeper level than ever before.

We have all experienced something that has broken us, and we've made the repairs needed for us to survive and, in many cases, thrive. And just like that Japanese pottery, our breaks are what make us unique, precious, and valuable. They strengthen us and give us the wisdom that comes from working through the difficult times. And when we learn to accept those beautiful lessons, we are able to speak our truths and share them with others to help them repair their own breaks.

# Hurt People Hurt People

was a pretty horrible preteen and early teenager—never in public, but at home and with those who were closest to me. I had a hair-trigger temper and would often erupt for no apparent reason. Sometimes that eruption was physical in nature, like the time I threw the television remote at my younger sister and cut her head. I certainly didn't mean to, and I don't think I was actually aiming for her. But at the time, this action seemed like the only way to get out some of the anger, frustration, and resentment that was building inside of me for reasons I couldn't understand.

Looking back now, with all I have learned since then, I can give a myriad of explanations as to why I was having those feelings. Along with the usual teen angst of trying to figure out who I was and how I fit into my constantly changing world, I also had unresolved trauma that I didn't know how to deal with or make sense of.

Back then, though, all I knew was that I was hurting deeply. And because I didn't understand why I was feeling this way—and in some cases didn't even understand *what* was causing the turmoil and pain—I didn't have any way to deal with it. So it boiled over from time to time in a way that hurt others, sometimes physically but more often emotionally.

When we are hurting, we tend to express it in ways that are harmful to the people around us, ultimately creating more hurt. Some of the ways we might lash out include projecting our inner anger and pain onto family and close friends, usually because they are the safe ones who won't walk away; interpreting (or more often misinterpreting) other people's words or actions as meaning something negative about ourselves; alienating those we love and need the most; or erupting with inappropriate levels of emotion because something touched a nerve or triggered us.

It's only in the past ten years or so that I've done the inner work to understand my triggers, my emotional scars, and the imprints those early life experiences left on my identity and self-confidence. I can now more clearly understand how my own experiences, as well as those of others close to me, have all worked together. I've come to understand that the way that I react to my triggers, and even what those triggers might be, don't have a simple cause-and-effect explanation. And I've realized that our reactions and emotions don't just impact our own lives; they can affect anyone and everyone with whom we come into contact throughout our day. For example, when I'm hurting, I'm more likely to lash out with unkind words or act in an angry or passive aggressive way—or worse.

I can also see others through this new lens, which provides just a little understanding. For example, one significant adult figure in my life always managed to cut me down or disregard anything I had confidence or security in—whether that was an almost-perfect score on a math exam or a relationship with a beloved relative. Their comments made me question my ability, myself, and my very worth. But once I understood how my own hurt led to actions that would cut at others in the same way, I was able to see the ways in which this person was also hurt and understand that they were most likely insecure in their own way. That doesn't make what they did right—it only helps me extend a little grace to that person, and also to myself.

You see, people who have been emotionally or physically damaged tend to inflict their hurt and pain on others. We see examples of this in the news—and in our own lives—every day. A large percentage of those who have been sexually abused go on to abuse others. Those who suffered under an alcoholic parent often end up dealing with addiction themselves and afflicting the same behaviour on their own family.

The way hurt people behave, and even their reactions to others, often stems from past experiences that led them to certain beliefs about themselves and the world around them. These experiences have created a filter that colours the way they view, understand, and respond to the things that trigger those beliefs in order to protect their own broken places.

We've all experienced a time when a friend, family member, or colleague has had an excessive and hurtful response to a specific event. Many of us have also had times when we felt harshly or unfairly criticized or learned that someone else was complaining about us behind our backs. It can be easy—even natural—to take these actions personally, particularly when the person is coming at us in anger or in other hurtful ways. However, their actions are not about us at all; they're about what's inside them coming out and being projected onto others. The person is, at the most basic level, just protecting themselves and attempting to avoid mental and emotional pain.

This is why healing ourselves is so important. Our hurt and trauma will find a way to express themselves eventually, so we need be proactive and deal with them in a healthy manner. Otherwise, we will continue to cause ourselves, and others, even more hurt.

# Layers of Healing

I wish the healing process was a one-and-done type of thing—that once we'd done the hard work and found our peace, we'd be back to "normal," whatever that might be.

Disappointingly, healing ourselves is not a quick or easy journey. Just when we think we've got it all figured out, something triggers those difficult emotions or brings our unhealthy coping mechanisms back to the surface and we find ourselves right back in the middle of needing to do the work again.

When we start our healing journey—particularly for the bigger losses and deeper traumas in our lives—we begin with what we see on the surface: the emotions that have been overtaking our ability to have peaceful relationships, the habits and coping mechanisms that have helped bring us through the most difficult times, and often the health issues that are starting to show up as a result of those first two aspects. This is a great place to start, and these are often the most pressing things to deal with, but the improvements we make won't last if we don't keep pushing deeper.

I decided to take that six-week trip to deal with my own burn-out and to replace some bad habits with good ones. However, that was really just scratching the surface of everything I needed to deal with—the issues that were most pressing in that moment. That retreat helped me change many things in my life and come back with more focus and energy than I'd had in a long time, but it didn't take long for me to start falling back into old habits. When the next big trauma came along, my resolve quickly eroded as I simply tried to make it through the day.

To truly rid ourselves of our bad habits and coping mechanisms, we need to realize that many of them were developed to get us through the most difficult times. They played a role in keeping us safe—or, at the very least, making us feel safer. So, when we feel *unsafe*, those activities, emotions and patterns can kick in again without us even thinking about it.

One of my coping mechanisms started when I was just a toddler, right after the tragic death of my parents. Overnight, everything in which I would have found safety, security, and comfort was gone— my home, my parents, my pet, perhaps my stuffed animals or a special blanket. Everything. Not only that, but my sister and I were now living in a home filled with tension and immense grief because all the adults around us were also dealing with the loss of their friends, family, or children.

Understandably, I was distraught and inconsolable, and the adults around me were dealing with all the same emotions. So, the adults did whatever they could do to bring some calm and quiet. Sure, there may have been some distractions with a new toy or even a television program, but most of the time they resorted to handing me a cookie or some other snack. It brought everyone a few moments of peace so they could collect their own thoughts and emotions and figure out what came next.

Just to be clear, in no way am I trying to assign blame or fault. We do the best we can in any given situation, particularly when we are just trying to get through another day. Nobody could have known that I was learning my emotions weren't safe—that they made other people upset or uncomfortable. Nobody could have known that I was learning to stuff down those emotions with something that brought that dopamine or serotonin hit, like sugary snacks. Nobody could have known that this would develop into a disordered eating pattern that re-emerged every time a trauma or upsetting memory triggered it. Nobody could have known that it would take me years to figure out those patterns and understand their impact on my life.

Because that's the nature of coping with trauma. We develop patterns of being, reacting, and behaving in an effort to manage all those overwhelming and uncomfortable emotions. This may include substance abuse, addictive behaviours, emotional outbursts, retreating from everyone and everything, or all of these and more.

In my case, the binge eating I used to "stuff down" uncomfortable emotions led to weight issues, which then led to health issues. And when those health issues got to the point that I couldn't ignore them anymore, the healing process started. However, while I started by addressing the most urgent issues—my high blood pressure and blood sugar levels—through improving my diet and getting more exercise, I needed to go deeper than that. After all, these concerns were a result of my weight issues, which were in turn the result of the binge eating.

But what about the causes of the binging? Well, that was another layer to deal with, and it took some deeper work. Because even if we want to stop a destructive behaviour, the behaviour itself is also a symptom. Again, in my case, it was because binging was a learned coping strategy to get rid of or numb (or very literally *stuff down*) uncomfortable emotions.

I put so much effort into ridding myself of these emotions that it took time for me to even recognize what I was feeling. And when I *could* identify those emotions—anger, grief, sadness—then another layer of healing was opened up to me. I could finally recognize the deeper emotions of rejection and abandonment (or fear of both) that came from that early life trauma, and I could see how they impacted my behaviour.

Our surface behaviours are usually just that—the surface. But just like a simple home repair can reveal a bigger, more costly problem that needs to be fixed, there is always more for us to understand and discover when it comes to our stories. More than once I've done the work to heal one of these layers and believed that I was finally done with the hard work, only to be triggered once again and have something come up that needed a little more healing work. Because those patterns run deep.

I know this can sound overwhelming and difficult. And it is, but it also isn't, because we don't start with the deepest work. We start on that top layer—the things that need the most immediate attention, like urgent health issues—and then work on one layer at a time. By taking this approach, the process becomes so much more manageable.

The key here is to build trust. Trust in ourselves and our ability to work through our experiences to better understand our reactions and behaviours. Trust in any professional we bring in to help us, whether it's a physician, a nutritionist, a personal trainer, or therapist—or all of them! And trust that the work will be worth it, and that we *can* find healing.

Finally, we must always remember that this is *not* a one-and-done process. We are always learning and growing and experiencing new things. Sometimes, those things are difficult, and they may show us new areas that need a little work. That's okay. In those moments, we must remind ourselves of how far we've come, and then we continue the work of becoming our best selves.

# Understanding Our Emotions

When we are experiencing difficult emotions, many of us try to escape them by numbing ourselves through substance abuse, gambling, shopping, eating, and more. We rarely let what we consider to be negative emotions escape—that is, until the pressure has built up so much that they *have* to be released.

These "negative" emotions are the ones that are generally considered inappropriate or impolite: grief, sadness, resentment, outrage, fury, disgust, and more, though many of these could fall under the more general term of anger. We learn at an early age that the way we express ourselves will not only affect how the world views us, but also how other people treat us, so we learn to hide any emotions that make people uncomfortable in whatever way we can.

However, internalizing an emotion doesn't make it go away. We can push it aside for a short time, but it will continue to simmer beneath the surface. Anger in particular finds a way out eventually—either actively, with the person verbally or physically lashing out, or passively, with the person sulking or showing passive-aggressive behaviours. And often, this anger is a mask for deeper hurt, fear, and pain.

The biggest issue that comes from denying these completely human emotions—from ignoring or suppressing or internalizing any of them—is that they can end up hurting us even more. Why? Because they can lead to other, bigger issues such as illness, lowered self-worth, and inappropriate behaviour. In order to break the cycle, we have to learn how to express these emotions in a healthy way.

Our stories, and what we tell ourselves about our stories, can sustain or create anger, especially if we see ourselves as having been victimized or wronged. However, if we begin to ask ourselves what is triggering that anger, we can shift our perspective by discovering our strength or resiliency in the face of these difficult events. Making this shift or change isn't easy, and it can take time. Sometimes a lot of time. But if we can learn to see our stories from a place of compassion—a place of trying to understand all the elements, events, and perspectives that added to our experiences—we can soften these intense feelings. And when we do that, we can move out of the hurt and trauma of the past.

This is the case for all the so-called negative emotions that we associate with our traumas, our tragedies, or even the less intense stories we tell ourselves. When we get stuck in that emotional cycle, we stop ourselves from learning from the situation and moving on with our lives. So, the more we understand the source of our emotions, the more we understand the situation that created them and why we respond to the world the way we do. We can then use that understanding to guide our actions and our healing, learning something about ourselves that then becomes part of our story—the part that will help and inspire someone else.

One example of how releasing our emotions can heal our stories comes from Emily, one of the co-authors in the collaborative book project *The Gift in Your Story*. When she wrote her first draft, she quite literally spilled all her thoughts and emotions out onto the page along with the facts of her experience. It was honest, raw, vulnerable, and incredibly difficult for others to read. Emily hadn't yet found healing in her story; she was still caught up in the hurt, anger, and devastation of what had happened to her.

However, this process was a necessary first step. Emily had been feeling all these emotions but had kept them hidden inside for years, and it had been affecting her health and well-being. She had been experiencing difficulty sleeping, high stress, weight loss, and more. Getting her story out on paper, along with her emotions, allowed Emily to begin the healing process, because just writing everything down was a release in itself. For probably the first time in her life, she decided she needed to put herself first—her needs, her desires, and her well-being.

After writing that first draft, Emily was able to start the deeper work. She removed herself from her everyday life and went somewhere she had always wanted to go: Santa Fe, New Mexico. She surrounded herself with healers and healing energy, and she wasn't afraid to do the hard work and confront her own role in the dysfunction of the past several years. She also poured her heart and emotion into her art.

This process wasn't quick; Emily immersed herself in the work of healing for several months. But as she did, her story changed. It went from being full of anger, pain, and resentment to sharing the peace she had found and acknowledging all she had to be grateful for. She not only healed herself, but she also created the opportunity to facilitate healing in others.

# Being Cracked Open

Sometimes, the smallest things can crack open a place in us that we didn't know needed healing—a part of our experience that is integral to our story and needs to be given attention before we can move forward.

These moments can be triggered by all kinds of experiences—a book, a television show, a movie, or even a passing comment. Often, they are an indication of the bigger stories in our lives, the ones we automatically think of whenever we consider whether we have a story to share. These are the difficult stories, the emotionally heavy ones. They are the ones that bring about the most change in us and in the people who have the privilege to hear them.

We never know what it is that could crack those places open in us. It simply happens when we're ready—and sometimes, when we least expect it.

One of my first experiences with being broken open came thanks to a toddler. Children of this age have not yet learned the art of hiding their emotions. They are real, raw, and sometimes brutally honest. There is no pretense with them. They are often more present and in the moment than any adult can be. They haven't learned how to be subtle and don't think before they speak or act. If you've spent any time at all around toddlers, you know exactly what I mean.

This particular event took place at the Malibu Club, one of the most formative places of my early adulthood. Malibu is a Young Life camp in British Columbia, Canada, that welcomes teenagers from

42

around North America through the summer months to experience "the best week of their lives."

I attended this camp the summer after eleventh grade, and then the next summer I was chosen to be part of a three-week volunteer work crew. My main assignment was to work in the camp's retail store doing things like folding shirts, restocking shelves, and of course, serving customers. The store manager lived at the camp for the whole season, along with her husband—who was the property manager—and their three children, whom I would help care for. That summer the eldest was five, the middle child was two, and the youngest was just a few months old.

As I got to know the family, I discovered that we lived in the same city. So, once the summer was over, I also became one of their regular babysitters and got to know them all even better.

The next summer, the family invited me back up to camp at the beginning of the season to help with the kids while their mother set up the store and trained the staff. The kids (now six, three, and one) would generally have breakfast with their parents in their camp home. Then the eldest would spend time in the store with her mother while the boys and I hung out on the sandy beach, played games, ate lunch, and had fun. For dinner, I would take them into camp where they would eat with all the other staff kids, with their parents sometimes joining us. More often than not in those first few days, I would then take the kids back to their home and put them to bed at the end of the day.

Needless to say, after a couple of busy days preparing the camp to open after a long winter season, the children hadn't seen much of their parents— just a few minutes here and there each day. One day, the three-year-old in particular was really missing his mother. I was able to keep him occupied with games and activities for most of the morning, but just after lunchtime (likely because he was tired and ready for a nap) he fell apart. And when I say he fell apart, I mean he lost it. He wanted his mommy, and nothing else was going to be good enough. He was crying and yelling, getting so worked up that he started hyperventilating. There was nothing I could do to calm him down, absolutely nothing. He was inconsolable.

I can't remember whether he cried himself out and finally fell asleep out of exhaustion or if I had to get his mother to come out and spend some time with him. I *do* remember that I felt a little overwhelmed—not from him or his intense level of upset, but from the effect it was having on me. I wasn't even sure what was going on or why I was feeling this emotional tumult.

As the afternoon progressed, my thoughts started to come together. My mind began to connect his inconsolable distress with the fact that my parents died when I was the very same age. And not only had they disappeared from my life, but my environment was also completely different because the only home I had ever known was gone, along with all the things that were familiar to me. My dog. My toys. My sources of comfort. There was no possibility of seeing my mother at the beginning of the day when I just woke up. No greeting from my father at the end of the workday. No bedtime routine of stories or prayers or being tucked in by one or both of them. They were just gone. And my three-year-old brain and emotions wouldn't have known how to make sense of it all—how to understand what death was and what it meant. All I would have known was that they weren't there.

So, if this little boy was so upset after just two days of seeing very little of his mother, how completely traumatized and inconsolable must I have been? And there wouldn't have been any relief to that upset because my mother or father couldn't show up to comfort me.

After this realization, I was so caught up in my own thoughts and emotions that I missed dinner. While the whole camp was eating, I sat by myself, looking out over the water, and let the emotions flow unchecked. The tears started slowly, but soon the full weight of the realization and understanding hit me and I became that toddler, sobbing uncontrollably in a way I never remembered doing before. I even called out, just like that little boy. "I want my mommy! Where's my daddy?"

This release was painful—not only emotionally, but also physically and spiritually. I could feel it at a visceral level. These emotions needed to empty from a place deep inside my soul where they had been buried for more than fifteen years, and I couldn't stop them if I wanted to.

I don't have any idea how long I sat there, letting the grief and sorrow and despair drain out. I wondered for a time if the end would ever come—it seemed as though each wave was followed by another. But eventually those waves became smaller and smaller as my emotional storm blew itself out for the day. As the tension ebbed, there was also something resembling peace starting to appear. That's not to say this piece of my life was forever healed—early life tragedy and trauma like that will have a much more far-reaching effect in our lives. Instead, the healing and understanding had finally been allowed to start. And all because these emotions were brought to the surface by a three-year-old whose experiences in the moment spoke to my own three-year-old self. The freedom and safety he felt to fully express his emotions were a much-needed catalyst to crack open that sewn-up place within me.

Be open to these catalysts in your own life because they point the way to some of your most important growth. Often, you are drawn to another's story because it has something for you—something that you need to take that next step in your own journey. Whether it brings out your empathy and compassion, reveals your emotions, or even highlights a place that needs healing in your own life, it'll help you take that next (or first) step toward healing.

# The Power of Forgiveness

We all have unique reactions to being wronged. Some of us may try to pick up the pieces and carry on as though nothing happened. Some may get stuck in the moment and find it difficult to move on. Some may use coping mechanisms to numb the pain. All these responses have something in common: not actually facing or dealing with the emotions involved.

Every challenging event has strong emotions attached to it: anxiety, anger, depression, frustration, fear, loneliness, isolation, powerlessness, the list goes on and on. The biggest problem with not expressing and releasing these emotions is that they have the potential to become toxic and destructive. You see, when we suppress these kinds of emotions, they create other things within us—things like stress and anxiety or other forms of upset. When we carry that stress, anxiety, and upset around, we tend to make our own health a lower priority. And when we don't take care of our health—physically *and* emotionally—we can actually weaken our body's immune system, making us more susceptible to viruses, illnesses, and even infection. That's quite the domino effect, isn't it?

We've all heard some version of the quote attributed to Buddha about how holding on to resentment is like drinking poison and waiting for the other person to die. Another version describes it as touching or holding fire and hoping someone else gets burned. The reason we've all heard these sayings is because they're true. Keeping up the hostility, aggression, and even passive-aggression that is needed to maintain resentment takes a significant amount of mental and emotional energy. It also creates a harmful cycle: the anger leads to negativity, which then creates more anger and on and on.

In order to let go of this anger and resentment, we must learn to forgive. This is the act of releasing the desire to punish someone—or even yourself—for an offense.

One important thing to note is that choosing to forgive does not mean forgetting and moving on, nor does it mean that the other person is absolved of the consequences of their actions. Instead, the act of forgiveness is choosing to release the desire for punishment or revenge, and it is only through this release that we can once again find peace of mind. It is more for you than it is for them.

Practicing forgiveness provides many benefits to our bodies, minds, and spirits. It helps us overcome our rage, anxiety, and depression; it allows us to find a sense of peace; it improves mental health and self-esteem; and ultimately, it helps us create healthier and stronger relationships.

Forgiveness is also important because when we hold on to hurt, pain, resentment, and anger, we harm ourselves more than the other person. Doing this keeps us in that negative cycle of anger and stress, which can lead to all kinds of health issues. When we can forgive and let go of those toxic emotions, we are free to live in the present and pursue our own growth and happiness.

Forgiveness isn't easy, and it isn't immediate. Achieving it means recognizing that your own mental and emotional health are more important than holding on to that anger, resentment, frustration, fear, or whatever emotion you're stuck on. And let me stress again that it is not about forgetting and moving on. It's about taking back your own power and valuing yourself. It's about considering yourself and your long-term health and happiness as being more important than what that person did.

Of course, forgiving is definitely way easier said than done! It's not so simple as just deciding to "let it go," as the song goes.

It starts with just choosing to forgive. This can't be forced; you have to *want* to move on and get to a more peaceful place. When we release the desire to punish the other person, to understand the reasons behind their actions, we can start to release our own emotional attachment to the incident.

Allowing ourselves to truly feel all the emotions related to this event is an important part of the process. When we do this, it becomes easier to consider how these emotions have been affecting us in all our other interactions and relationships. Perhaps the anger is causing us to have a shorter fuse with our family, our kids, or even strangers. Perhaps the hurt, sadness, and betrayal are making us avoid creating deeper relationships with others.

Once you've reached this understanding, it becomes easier to find some perspective and empathy regarding both the situation and the other person or people involved. Often, it also helps us be more aware of just how much other people may be hurting.

In fact, as we allow ourselves to feel compassion for others, even those who have wronged us, we begin to release the emotions that are harming us. And as we become more aware of our own wounds and the wounds that we all carry, we become more patient with others—and with ourselves.

Unfortunately, as much as I wish it were so, all those emotions and upset are not going to just disappear overnight, nor will the other person magically call or email to apologize just because we have chosen to forgive. This is the hardest part: letting go of any expectations and not taking the person's actions—or inaction—personally. We all make mistakes, all say and do things we later regret. And we have all been hurt.

And as I have said, hurt people hurt people.

But you can't change other people; you can only change yourself. Make a choice to learn from the experience and begin surrounding yourself with people who build others up instead of tearing them down. Also, forgive yourself for any feelings of misplaced trust or naïveté in allowing that person into your life in the first place.

Forgiveness is more about us than it is about the other person. When we can forgive—both others and ourselves—then the healing can really begin.

# Stop Should-ing on Yourself

One of the biggest stumbling blocks we face when coming to terms with our own stories is a pervasive undercurrent of guilt and, in many cases, shame. Many events in our lives—the difficult ones in particular—come with a lot of self-judgment about the things we could or should have done or said to ensure a different outcome. About the words we left unsaid before a loved one's passing. About the calls we didn't make to mend a broken friendship. Even about the sunscreen we should have applied every time we went out in the sun!

When that false guilt is lurking under the surface, it makes finding and claiming the lesson in our story—or gift, as I like to call it—more difficult. We get stuck in a never-ending cycle of self-judgment, regret, shame, and guilt, which makes us feel even worse about ourselves and our actions or non-actions.

To understand this concept more fully, it would probably help to start with a description of the difference between real and false guilt.

True or healthy guilt is the guilt you feel when you have actually done something wrong. Maybe you were rude to the barista at your favourite coffee shop because you just got some bad news *and* you'd been waiting in line for longer than expected *and* you were running late for work. Or you spent hours on the phone trying to get through to a real person at your phone or cable company, and you dumped your frustration and anger on the first person you spoke with.

True guilt serves a purpose. The remorse and discomfort we feel hopefully pushes us to apologize or make things right—to do what it takes to repair that relationship. Ultimately, true guilt comes from our actions not lining up with our internal sense of integrity—from doing something we know is wrong based on our own values. This guilt is reasonable and appropriate, and the mature response is to be accountable for our actions and make amends.

False guilt, on the other hand, is unreasonable, inappropriate, and unhealthy. At its core, false guilt is about blaming yourself. It is most often triggered by something external, perhaps a demand or standard—even a self-imposed one—that you did not or could not meet. And often, we can't meet these demands because we are doing what we need to do in order to take care of ourselves. Maybe you postponed a coffee date with a friend because your schedule was overloaded and it was adding to your stress. Maybe you took a weekend off to sleep and read a novel because your mind needed the break from the intensity and stress of work. Maybe you indulged in a sweet treat when you were committed to following a diet. False guilt is most often associated with not feeling worthy enough to make yourself a priority or take care of your own well-being.

The biggest problem with false guilt is that making amends doesn't relieve those guilty feelings, which then leads to self-judgment, then back to false guilt, and so on and so on. Sound familiar? There's that cycle again.

So, how do we tell the difference between true and false guilt? When you're experiencing true guilt, you know exactly why you're feeling it. You can see the entire cycle of actions that led you to this place, and taking action to fix the situation eases the guilt and allows you to forgive yourself. On the other hand, when you're experiencing false guilt, you are protecting someone else's feelings. You feel out of control, stuck, or trapped, and the guilt is not eased by attempting to make amends.

Another way to determine if you're feeling false or true guilt is to figure out what words and phrases you are using in your self-talk around the situation. In particular, are you using the word "should": I should have said this instead of that, I should have made time for this person, I should have studied harder for that test, I should have thought of that before I said what I did, I should have gone to that family dinner, called that friend, volunteered at that event.

"Should" is a trigger word that creates those feelings of guilt. When we "should" on ourselves, we get stuck in that self-judgment cycle and feel even worse about ourselves than usual. We judge ourselves against an unrealistic standard and blame ourselves for falling short of that made-up expectation. This is unhealthy because it often comes in response to prioritizing our own health and well-being. We feel thoughtless and selfish, and we get caught up in that destructive cycle, repeating the same "shoulds" over and over again.

This false guilt—or should-ing on ourselves—actually hinders us in claiming the truth of our own stories. It's the rape victim telling herself that she *should* have dressed differently or had less to drink or not stayed out so late and then this wouldn't have happened to her. Maybe some of this comes from societal manipulations, but either way, blaming herself has become her inner dialogue.

It's the person trying to lose weight beating themselves up for not sticking perfectly to their plan. They *should* have gone to the gym or should have avoided that piece of cake at their best friend's party. They *should* have more willpower, and this should be easy. This is expecting perfection and denying the reality that life happens, and that nobody can be perfect all the time.

It's the parent who stays late at work to meet a deadline who keeps thinking they *should* be home with their family, and they *should* be tucking their kids into bed. Conversely, it's the parent missing an important deadline because they went home to be with their family thinking they *should* have worked thirty minutes later each day that week, or they *should* be further ahead in their career. It's getting too focused on our expectations of what being successful in the workplace and as a parent looks like, leading to guilt on either side.

It is me thinking I *should* have been better behaved as a toddler. I *should* have listened to my mother the first time she asked me to do something, I *should* have had fewer tantrums, and then my parents wouldn't have died. It's ridiculous, but deep down in my subconscious, I actually thought this was true. My mature, adult mind knows that my (very normal) actions as a toddler had absolutely nothing to do with my parents falling asleep while they were smoking, and yet those thoughts persisted for *years*. But that's the problem with false guilt: it isn't reasonable, and it doesn't make rational sense, which makes it all the more difficult for us to stop the cycle.

We have responsibilities, both to ourselves and to others, and we have to take accountability for our actions. But when we're feeling guilty about something, we have to recognize when those messages are about our actual actions—actions we can change or apologize for—or are about telling ourselves how selfish or thoughtless we are.

Imagine how much lighter, freer, and happier we would feel if we could stop all this should-ing on ourselves. And it *is* possible, though it does take some time and effort.

Start by noticing how often you use the word "should" when describing any actions you did or didn't take (or words you did or didn't say). Then, when you catch yourself in these negative cycles, take some time to notice what is going on underneath the surface and figure out the truth of the situation. Think about it from the point of view of an unbiased observer—what are the facts involved rather than the emotions?

Then, ask yourself: who is the one actually causing this self-blame? Your inner critic? Societal messages or expectations? Perhaps even a person who might be using these things to manipulate your behaviour? You could also take a good look at the reason for your guilt. Does it make rational sense? Did you do something for which you could apologize or make amends? The answer to these questions will help you determine if you are experiencing true or false guilt.

Finally, practice self-compassion and self-acceptance. Many of these irrational expectations we put on ourselves are well-worn thought patterns that were formed early in our lives. It takes time to remake those paths so that you can take care of yourself and your own needs without feeling selfish. Give yourself that time, and give yourself space to not always get it right.

When we release all the false guilt we often carry around without even knowing it, we not only free ourselves from the weight of those inherent expectations but also allow ourselves to see our stories in a clearer light. That's when we can find the gift we received from each and every experience, which we can then share with others. And that's when our stories can—and do—make a difference.

# How Our Secrets Make Us Sick

Recently, I went on a month-long road trip. I planned the stops I wanted to take, the places I wanted to see, the people I wanted to connect with, and the weather I hoped to find! Living in a temperate rain forest means a lot of grey, rainy days, so I was craving some sunshine.

Overall, the trip was great. But a few hours after I arrived home, I received a text from my brother: "Welcome home sis! I just wanted to let you know that your nephew had an accident while you were away. We chose not to let you know as we didn't want to ruin your trip or cause you to end your trip early, especially after the doctors told us that they believe all would be okay. He crashed his dirt bike and as a result fractured his neck..." The text went on to detail his injuries and asked me to "please not be mad at anyone" for not telling me.

Understandably, I was upset. My eldest nephew had broken his neck, and nobody told me! But as I thought about it, my family members were right. Had I known about it when the accident happened, I would have figured out a way to get home as quickly as possible to ensure, with my own eyes, that he was going to be okay. In fact, when I realized the day it happened—with two weeks left in my trip—I knew exactly what I would have done. A friend was visiting me as I was staying a couple of hours from her home. I would have followed her back to her home, left my car there, and taken the first flight I could. Not only would I have been ending my trip early, but I also would have been distraught and not in the right frame of mind to be behind the wheel as I drove the miles to my friend's home. So yes, they had made the right decision in keeping the secret of his accident while I was away.

As I processed this experience, I began thinking about the secrets we keep, and how there are positive and negative sides to them.

I think when we decide to keep a secret, it's often with the best of intentions. It comes from a place of love and care, wanting to avoid causing emotional pain to another. In this case, my family knew me well enough to predict that I would want to drop all my travel plans to get home as quickly as possible. And considering that I was more than two thousand kilometers away, it would also mean that I would be driving some very busy freeways and roads in a less-than-ideal emotional state, or that I would somehow otherwise alter my plans to get home even faster by airplane. They also knew that my nephew was very likely (and very fortunately) going to have a full recovery, and they had every intention of telling me as soon as I arrived home.

There are other secrets that similarly start out with the best of intentions. However, the longer these secrets are kept, the higher the possibility of unintended consequences.

These are the secrets that we keep (or that are kept from us) that ultimately result in eliciting feelings of shame. In her book *Daring Greatly*, Brené Brown defines shame as "the intensely painful feeling or experience of believing that we are flawed and therefore unworthy of love and belonging." She also sets shame apart from guilt by explaining that while guilt is the consequence of having *done* something bad, shame is *being* something bad or unworthy.

How does that relate to our secrets? Well, think about the secrets we keep, or those that perhaps were kept from us. For example, in the first months and years of losing my parents and being adopted into a new family, I remember mentioning that my parents had died in a fire. My adoptive mother quickly told me that it was NOT a fire that had taken their lives, and then changed the subject. I never brought it up again because I had been told I was wrong. It wasn't until I was in my early twenties that my grandmother reluctantly told me what happened, after stating that she wasn't even sure she was supposed to tell me.

Wanting the full story, I headed to the library to search the archives for old newspaper articles about their death. Since I knew the year and the approximate date, I searched files and files of microfiche until I came across the article detailing the tragedy. And the article said there was a fire that had been started late at night by a dropped cigarette.

So why did my adoptive mother tell me that there wasn't a fire? I never did ask her, so I'll never know for sure. But looking back now, I remember that for the first several days and weeks after this incident, I was having terrifying nightmares that would have me inconsolable and searching for any adult who could reassure me. I believe my mother thought that by denying there was a fire, she was helping remove an element that was causing my nightmares (and also causing interrupted sleep for others in the house). She was doing the best she could in a very emotional and difficult situation, trying to solve the most immediate issue.

The problem is that when we're missing necessary information, we will naturally fill in the blanks with whatever makes the most sense to us in that moment. So, when I thought (and was told) that I was wrong about the fire, I then wondered what *had* taken my parents away. And the only other thing that made sense to me was that I had done something wrong, that I was somehow not good enough or unworthy. (Bear with me here, this is a toddler's reasoning.) And because nobody ever talked about the event that changed our lives, I felt that I would only upset others if I asked questions about it. Instead, I kept it inside and decided to do anything I could to prove to myself and others that I was worthy of having parents, of having a family, of being loved.

This is just one example of a secret having unintended but damaging consequences. My mother's decision to hide the truth had an effect on me that lasted for years, often resulting in feeling as though I wasn't good enough or that I had to prove myself—something I've been battling most of my adult life.

There are a lot of other things that we keep secret, often because of the stigma that our society attaches to them. Things like rape, assault, being scammed or catfished, and even mental health challenges like anxiety, disordered eating, depression, and ADHD to name just a few. Why do we keep these things secret? Because we feel some level of shame about them. We feel that there's something inherently wrong with us or within us that has caused us to face these issues and challenges. We also feel that if we admit them or bring them out into the light, then we are somehow admitting that we are unworthy of love and acceptance.

The truth is that these things do not make us unworthy or unlovable or somehow wrong. And the even bigger truth is that the minute we bring them out of the darkness and start sharing these struggles and challenges with people we trust, our shame starts to lose its grip on us.

One such secret of my own has recently found its way back to the surface in my own life. In my twenties, I started having extreme anxiety over some of my early life trauma. It manifested in many ways, but mainly in sleeplessness, which in turn influenced my mood and my desire to even interact with others. I was still going through all the motions of managing my work life and even a minimal social life, but for more than three months I spent at least an hour of every day in tears. There was so much pain surfacing that I felt I just couldn't bear it for another day.

So, I decided I would end it all and take my own life so that I didn't have to feel this pain for another day. I started planning how I would do it, and when. I honestly didn't think anyone would even miss me.

Obviously, since I'm telling you this now, I didn't go through with my plans. But what's most important about this glimpse into my pain is that at the time, I never told anyone just how bad things were or what I had planned. I eventually told one person, but then I buried it. Why? Because the word "suicide" carries such stigma that I felt ashamed of even contemplating it. It was only after another recent round of work and healing that I have decided to start sharing this story with others.

When I first made the decision to talk about it, I couldn't even say the word suicide. I talked about choosing to leave this life, or ending the pain, or just "leaving." But what I started to realize was that the more I used the word "suicide" and talked about the circumstances around my experiences, the less stigma and shame I felt. And the more I shared this story and the associated realizations, clarity, and even healing I was experiencing, the more others felt able to share their own similar feelings and experiences with me.

It's the same with every other area in which we feel and experience shame. The more we talk about it, the more it loses its power over us, and the more we can find the healing that is so essential to living a full and fulfilling life.

# Acknowledging Our Judgment

A few years ago, I hosted The Power of Story Conference here in Vancouver. This one-day event featured a variety of people sharing their stories of discovering their paths and overcoming the challenges they have faced, as well as talking about why our stories are so important to discover and share. I started things off by asking all the attendees to look around at the people sitting beside them, behind them, even across the room from them. Then I said that without even knowing it, they each had likely made micro-judgments about one or more of those people— things like noticing an expensive purse and deciding that person is well-off or believing that someone else's purple hair means they are a rebel.

Because it's true.

We, as humans, have a constant need to classify everything and everyone we come into contact with. Back in caveman days, lives were lost or saved based on many of those instinctual judgments. Friend or foe? Safe or poisonous?

However, in today's culture, these judgments don't serve the same purpose. We know that *most* of the people who cross our paths aren't going to threaten our safety or our lives. We also shop in grocery stores where we know the products are safe to consume—or at least are not going to kill us within the next few days. But just like we can't know at a glance what nutrients a food contains, we also don't know who a person really is until we take the time to find out who they really are.

One summer, I was heading out to volunteer for six weeks at Malibu Club, that Young Life camp I mentioned before. There were fifty of us all coming to work together for the session, and we had an eight-hour boat ride to get to the camp. At one point, we were all in a circle introducing ourselves, and I made some kind of impression on everyone else, just as they did on me. And even now, more than twenty years later, I remember a few things from those initial introductions: the outgoing, boisterous girl; the guy who didn't like having his name shortened; the girl with the quirky style and her incredible hat. And through these impressions, I formed an opinion on who I thought these people were.

Fast forward to the end of the first week, and I'd had the chance to have some real interactions and conversations with many of these people. We'd chopped vegetables and made bread together. We'd swept boardwalks and pulled weeds. We'd made beds and cleaned windows and shared meals. And when I thought back to those initial introductions? I didn't even recognize some of them as the same people that I'd now had the opportunity to get to know. I'd learned something about their story—where they came from, what their experiences had been throughout grade school and high school, what their family was like, maybe even something about the hobbies they loved.

This was my first real lesson on not judging a book by its cover.

I'm sure I've provided the same lesson for others because even on my worst days, not many people would have ever known something was wrong. I would still smile and say good morning to anyone I passed when walking my dog. I would still say please and thank you when ordering my latte at the coffee shop down the street. I would still go to work and interact with my colleagues, clients, and suppliers. I would still make myself available to a friend if they needed a listening ear or a shoulder to cry on.

However, anyone who looked close enough may have been able to see the cracks. My smile might have faltered with that "good morning." I might have been somewhat impatient with the cashier or barista. I could have been abrupt or short with my colleagues because my mind wasn't fully on the question they asked or the potential problem they had encountered. And while I definitely would have listened to my friend, I might not have been actually hearing and understanding what they were saying because of the flood of thoughts in my head.

Each one of those people—the neighbor, the barista, the co-worker, the friend—very likely formed a thought or judgment about me based on that momentary interaction. They may have found me welcoming, friendly, demanding, dismissive, uncaring, or any number of things based on that instant in time. The friend is likely to call me out on not listening and ask what's going on because they know me and what's going on in my life—particularly the things that are taking most of my emotional and mental energy at that time. But the others? They don't know the bigger picture. Maybe I'm struggling with my finances and wondering how I'll pay the bills at the end of the month. Or perhaps someone close to me has been given a terminal diagnosis and I'm trying to come to grips with the impending loss. Or maybe someone rear-ended my car on the way to work that morning and I've been dealing with increasing pain ever since.

My point? We never know what is truly going on with someone

unless we truly *know* that person—unless we have taken the time to ask them questions and discover a piece of their story.

It's not easy to stop these quick, snap judgments because they affect our own experience. If someone is rude to us, then we may be rude to the next person we talk to. If someone is dismissive of our ideas or experience, we may become more closed off from having an honest interaction with the next person. The only way to stop this domino effect is to start asking questions and practicing empathy. Find out more about who that person is. Put yourself in their shoes. Look past the cover and find the incredible story within.

# The Key is Connecting

W e live in a time when we are more connected with the world than ever before. And yet, as I mentioned earlier, we are also experiencing more loneliness than any other time in history.

One of the biggest problems is that many of us look at social connections as a numerical equation. We see that we have more than five hundred friends on Facebook or more than two thousand followers on Instagram and think, *How can I feel lonely? I have all these friends.*

The truth is that loneliness isn't determined by the actual number of friends or social contacts a person has. In fact, those friends or followers on social media apps don't count for anything, so stop looking at those as some kind of badge of honour or proof of popularity.

I have something of a love/hate relationship with social media. I love it because it's helped me connect with so many people from different times in my life: school friends with whom I'd lost touch, people from all over North America whom I worked with at Malibu Club, former colleagues from various jobs and organizations, and even people from around the world whom I've met through online courses. And as I shared earlier, it's because of social media that I was able to connect with the family of the man who saved me from that house fire when I was three years old, and to hear from others who were affected by that event. I likely would not have been touched by all these stories had it not been for social media.

However, the side I don't love as much, and perhaps even sometimes hate, is the side that falsely tells me I have all these "friends" when many of these people are little more than connections from a moment in time. Social media gives us the impression that we have so many people in our lives when the reality is often very different, and that's where the loneliness can come in.

Loneliness is defined as the emotional state created when people have fewer social contacts and meaningful relationships than they would like. The key here is *meaningful relationships*. These are the people that truly make us feel seen, heard, and understood. They help us grow, offer us support, encourage us, and are there for us when we need them. They help us thrive. And the number of *those* relationships in our lives isn't going to have a lot of zeroes behind it.

And if we don't have any of these kinds of relationships? That's when we find ourselves disconnected and lonely.

The biggest problem with loneliness is that it makes us sick. Most of us would agree that when we're lonely, we might feel sad or depressed or perhaps have low self-esteem. But physically sick? Believe it or not, it's true. Loneliness can take our health away—emotional, mental, *and* physical.

In fact, loneliness isn't just making us sick, it's killing us. The American Psychological Association states that loneliness has been found to increase our levels of stress, anxiety, and depression; impede our sleep; and ultimately harm our bodies. Loneliness can even increase our risk of having a heart attack by more than forty percent.

One cause of loneliness is that we are tuning out the world more and more, even while we *think* that we're more connected. How often do we leave the house without our smartphone in hand? Where do we keep it when we are working? Or cooking? Or doing any number of usual daily tasks? How about when we are with friends and family? We've all seen it and even done it ourselves: friends in a restaurant all on their phones instead of interacting. People looking down at the apps or playlists on their phones rather than greeting someone on the sidewalk. Tourists constantly looking through phone cameras for the next Instagram-worthy moment instead of being present and taking in the sights.

This is not entirely our fault; the truth is that our phones and their apps are actually created to facilitate addiction. You see, all the ways we interact with our phones and apps—particularly social media apps—develop an expectation of or desire for a reward. And that reward? The notifications of texts, likes, comments, and other such interactions. Each time we get a notification, it releases dopamine and lights up our brain, similar to what would happen if we took a recreational drug. That dopamine release is basically a bit of a hit of chemical happiness, and the more it happens, the more we want. That's the very nature of addiction.

Unfortunately, this happiness isn't based on anything real. Too often, what we are all sharing on social media is the best moments of our day or week. It's a snapshot in time that doesn't accurately reflect all that's going on in our lives. And these technology-based connections do not in any way replace the power of connecting with someone—anyone—in person.

We make connections anytime we have an interaction where one or more person comes away feeling inspired, encouraged, motivated, or even transformed and healed in some way. This could include having a conversation with a friend or relative, learning from a workshop or podcast, or even watching a documentary, movie, or other program. And yes, these moments can also happen on, or because of, social media. However, too often we look for those connections to be life-changing "a-ha moments," as Oprah coined them, rather than recognizing that sometimes even the simplest of interactions can make a difference in how we feel.

We don't have to connect with a meaningful person in our lives in order to receive benefits that scrolling through a newsfeed can't provide. Sometimes, even a look of understanding between two strangers can create a sense of belonging, which can then encourage us, boost our confidence, and make us feel less alone.

Being truly connected with others through real-life interactions generates a positive feedback loop of social, emotional, and physical well-being. And we can find these moments wherever we find ourselves in the day—a coffee shop, the line at the bank, a park, the grocery store, the list is endless!

Just by spending time socializing and connecting with others, we can reap the benefits of an improved mood: inspiration, motivation, decreased stress levels, and much more. And when we have the opportunity to share even a small part of our story, we come to see the ways our experiences connect us all on a deeper, more meaningful level.

# The Problem with Perfect

J udgment goes hand-in-hand with the expectation that we and others should be perfect—there's that should-ing again! However, the desire or expectation to be perfect can often keep us from moving forward with our goals and dreams, including sharing our stories. We often get stuck trying to find the perfect words or phrases to convey what we're trying to say. We also compare our stories to others' and decide that ours just isn't good enough to matter. Well, that's simply not true.

Wanting or striving for perfection isn't necessarily a bad thing, particularly when it helps us achieve a goal or advance in our career. Part of the reason I was able to produce so many successful events over the years is because I was trying to provide perfection for my clients. But when that pursuit becomes an all-or-nothing goal, one where we must be completely perfect or we have failed, then it begins to cause problems.

Let me give you a couple of examples. For one, I've wanted to paddleboard for years now—yes, years—and yet I've never done it. Why? Because I don't want to do it less than perfectly. I know a lot of people who paddleboard in any season, even fully clothed, because they know they'll stay on the board and stay dry. I'm pretty sure that I'll be in the water more often than not the first time I go out there, and assuming that I will "fail" more than I succeed stops me.

The same is true when it comes to anything around eating properly or dieting or clean eating, whatever phrase you prefer to use. I know that I'll feel like a failure if I can't do it perfectly all the time, and I let that fear of failing prevent me from starting, even though my rational mind knows that having it be all or nothing is a recipe for failure in itself. Not wanting or allowing myself to fail, in these areas and so many more, is a result of me being extremely hard on myself and expecting perfection.

And yes, in some tasks, perfection *is* possible. You could attain a perfect grade on a test or a perfect score in bowling. You could learn to make the perfect hard-boiled egg or cup of coffee or margarita or steak—at least the perfect one to suit your tastes. However, striving for perfection in *any* area often reminds us how very imperfect we are.

Do any of the situations below sound familiar to you? If so, then you are likely falling into the perfectionism trap.

- You decide that this is the year you are going to be as healthy as possible. So, you embark on a plan to eat only clean, whole, non-processed foods and do some form of exercise every day. The first few days go great, and you think, *I'm KILLING this! I'll be running a half marathon by the summer!* Then on day three or five or eight or twelve, you eat something off-plan or skip a day of exercise because of your workload or family obligations. This starts a downward spiral toward giving up completely because you are focused on that failure to stick with your plan.

- You want to cook healthy meals for your family, so you decide to invest in one of those meal kit companies that gets delivered to your door. Quick. Easy. Totally doable. And then one day, you're running from work to kids' activities to the gym to errands and you are *exhausted*. Just thinking about cooking—and cleaning up the mess afterwards—adds to the stress. Your spouse orders pizza or Chinese food or whatever your family's favourite greasy, fried, or carb-loaded take-out is. Another plan blows up.

- You recognize that you could be better managing your money, so you set a budget that should have you debt-free by the end of the year. But then something unexpected happens. You need new tires or brakes for your car, or your roof begins to leak, or your refrigerator breaks down, or any number of other things that cost money to repair or replace. Suddenly, all the progress you made in paying off your debts is wiped out. You feel defeated.

Did any of these resonate with you? I know they do for me. I can't tell you the number of times I've decided it's time to lose weight once and for all, because I've lost count. I tried Weight Watchers and Jenny Craig. I've paid for countless gym memberships and exercise programs. I've read books like *Fit for Life* and *The South Beach Diet*, plus all kinds of books on changing your mindset. I've studied the science around nutrition and exercise. I've tried so many different ways of eating—primal, paleo, keto, and more. And let's not forget trips to the health spa and personal trainers. I even had meal deliveries based on specific macronutrients for over six months.

All of these worked, for a while. But every time, something happened that led to what I considered to be failure. I tore a ligament in my ankle and had to stop my training. A holiday or family celebration came along and interrupted my diet. Christmas was the worst for this: there would be a month (and sometimes more) of constant temptations and parties, and suddenly I was moving backwards and once again feeling like a failure.

Why am I so demanding of and hard on myself? Because deep down, I've struggled with accepting my own worth.

I could point to several times in my life where this belief that I didn't measure up could have been formed. Being orphaned. Feeling left out because my jeans didn't have the right label, being teased because I had a bad haircut, or getting bullied for who knows what reason. Being criticized for only getting 99% on a math test or being ridiculed for auditioning for a role in a musical. So many of these experiences became the tapes that played over and over in my head, reinforcing the thought that I had to prove my value every day.

Eventually, my sense of self-worth was so low that I spent most days putting my own needs, wants, and desires aside in order to prioritize what someone else might need. I was always worried that the people I cared about would reject me if I did something wrong. If I didn't help them. If I failed them.

And that whole time—or at least most of it—I was failing myself in the most important ways. Failing to see that my value wasn't dependent upon what I could do for other people, but on just being the best me I could be. I didn't need to strive for perfection because achieving it is impossible. Not one single person out of the more than seven billion people on this planet is perfect. Even machines aren't perfect.

Our pursuit of perfection is often an attempt to compensate for feelings of insecurity or inadequacy. We feel as though we are not enough—not good enough, talented enough, attractive enough, athletic enough, smart enough, whatever it might be. We think of others as being better than us, and we become more sensitive to the judgments of others (and our own self-judgment). And quite often, those judgments are based on own perceptions rather than facts. This is because we compare ourselves to what we *think* others feel or have attained. We then believe that these people are judging us as falling short, when in truth they are almost certainly doing the same thing: comparing themselves to us and believing that they fall short in some way.

Another problem with seeking perfection is that we are never fully in the present moment. Instead, we spend our time measuring or grading ourselves, either by critiquing our mistakes from the past or worrying about what's to come. But the biggest problem with seeking and striving for perfection is that it relies on the opinions of others—and those opinions constantly change. Besides, no two people share all the same opinions on things like what makes the perfect coffee or steak, or even the perfect chocolate chip cookie!

So, how do we stop trying to be perfect? How do we stop hiding anything that doesn't fit whatever image we've created of what perfection looks like? Stop being our own worst critic? Stop constantly judging our physical appearance, emotional responses, ability to cook that perfect steak?

For one, we need to remember that every single person who has ever existed has made mistakes. In fact, mistakes serve a very important purpose, and that is to help us learn. Some of the greatest inventions of our modern world came from people making mistakes: the microwave, penicillin, the first implantable pacemaker, x-ray images,

Post-it Notes, even chocolate chip cookies and potato chips! Those last ones might be the tastiest mistakes ever.

We also need to find some compassion for ourselves. Practicing self-compassion gives us the space to grow, break, fall, get back up again, and heal. It allows us to learn from our past experiences and realize that those very mistakes are what have helped us make new discoveries and grow. It helps us stop comparing ourselves to others and learn to accept and appreciate our own abilities, talents, and skills—all those things that make up who we really are at our core and make us unique.

If you're wondering about how to start practicing self-compassion, a good place to begin is asking yourself what you would tell a friend in the same situation. Would you offer criticism and judgment? I highly doubt that. So, give yourself the same encouragement and care you would give that friend.

Also, start to practice letting go of who you think you should be. Work on not just accepting but embracing who you truly are—all the weird, wonderful, quirky, amazing parts that make you unique and special and totally *you*. Because when you spend your time trying to be like someone else, the world misses out on what you can offer.

So, that brings us back to you and your story. Has the desire to tell it perfectly been holding you back from starting? Have you been listening to the stories of others—or even reading parts of my story—and wondering how yours could ever measure up?

The truth is that I've felt the same way, and I let that stop me for over a decade. Even in writing this book, I've had to recognize that it will never be perfect. I know that the day it's published, there are going to be things I wish I had changed because I'm always learning and growing. And I've had to decide that it's okay for this book to be less than perfect. It will be perfectly imperfect.

Just like me. And just like you.

Life has thrown many of us a lot of difficult experiences. And the longer we are here on Earth, the truer that's going to become—just consider the recent global pandemic. We will all experience traumas. We will all experience intense grief. We will all struggle and be challenged many times in many ways. And all this is in no way a reflection of our worth or value.

Diamonds can only form under high temperatures and intense pressure, and our society values them greatly. We view them as a symbol of committed love, of worth, of success and achievement. You too have been through incredible challenges and intense pressure, whether that be trauma, tragedy, illness, or even acts of nature. And just like the diamond, these experiences point to your strength, your resilience, your determination, your love, and yes, even your value.

It's time to recognize just how valuable and worthy you are—not because you are perfect, but simply because you exist.

# Releasing Expectation

We all have expectations—both for ourselves and for others—and we all know how it feels when those expectations aren't met. We've been disappointed when the people we care about don't support us in the way we had hoped they would. We've been sad and maybe even angry or frustrated when people don't remember or acknowledge a special occasion, like our birthdays. We've even experienced regret, frustration, guilt, and shame when we fail to live up to our own expectations.

That's the problem with having expectations—we set ourselves up for disappointment. Why? Because we are hoping that something will happen—such as receiving a specific response from others—often without having a good reason to anticipate that result. We also tend to connect our happiness or contentment or success to the fulfillment of those expectations, despite having no way to ensure that they are met.

Of course, there may be times when we have good reasons to expect a certain result, and in those cases, we can take the necessary steps to achieve the desired outcome. For example, we may know from past experiences that praying or meditating for ten to fifteen minutes each morning makes us more content and productive the rest of the day, or that our morning latte makes us less grumpy and therefore happier. These are good expectations to have because they are ones *we* can control. However, we often have expectations that involve the actions of other people, and those are the ones that can become problematic.

I know you can easily think of examples in your own life where people didn't live up to your expectations, whether you realized you had them or not. Not only do situations like these result in disappointment, but they can also lead to shock, anger, and even resentment. And there is no part of our lives where these expectations are more abundant than in our relationships with the people we care about. Parents have expectations of their children, spouses have expectations of their partners, bosses have expectations of their employees. And vice versa. We have expectations in our friendships and even in our relationships with co-workers and clients.

These expectations are based on some kind of implicit social contract—if you care about me, you will meet my expectations. The problem is that these expectations aren't universal, yet they are rarely verbalized or talked about. We may have a preconstructed idea of how someone should relate to us, but we've never actually told the other person about it, which makes it hard for them to live up to our expectations. We need to stop expecting everyone to be able to read our minds and know exactly what we want and when we want it.

It's also often difficult for us to live up to our expectations for ourselves. We expect ourselves to be successful—in school, in sport, in our careers, in any goal we set. We might even have expectations about how we are going to reach those goals. Then we get paralyzed by the fear that we won't succeed as quickly as we should or in the way we think we should.

Do you see how easily our expectations get all tangled up with what we believe is the perfect path to success? There we go again, trying to be perfect and then feeling (falsely) guilty when we're not.

We have to stop expecting to be perfect and stop expecting every-one's path to be the same as our own. No two people are going to reach the same goal in exactly the same way, and no two stories are going to elicit the same response from the same listeners.

I remember my brother-in-law comparing expectations to base-ball—or more specifically, to a pitcher deciding what pitch to throw. He could choose a spitball, a curveball, a fastball, or possibly a change-up. But no matter how much thought he puts into this deci-sion, or how much knowledge he has about the batter standing in the box, he has absolutely no control over where the ball goes next. The batter could choose to bunt, or perhaps he times things perfectly and hits a home run. Once the ball leaves the pitcher's hand, it doesn't make much sense for him to have expectations of what happens next or be angry when they aren't fulfilled. When he releases the ball, he also needs to let go of any expectations and just be prepared for whatever comes back at him.

So, the question then becomes, how do we learn to release our expectations—especially those that we place upon others?

First, we need to become aware of our expectations. Think about what you expect from the world around you—from social situations, from events you attend, and from the people you care about. Some of these expectations might be realistic, but often they are based on long-held beliefs or stereotypes stemming from past experiences. They may even come from outdated societal beliefs—things like "men are the breadwinners" or "girls wear pink, boys wear blue" or "a university or college degree will guarantee me a good, high-pay-ing job." When you start to become aware of all the various expec-tations you hold, you can start to let go of any disappointment or anger around not having them met—mostly because you realize how unreasonable they were in the first place!

Second, we need to try seeing the world through the eyes of a child. Children approach every situation without expectation because it's all new to them, which means they have no idea what's going to happen next. If we work on trying to approach situations we've been in before as though they are new to us, we will then be able to appreciate the unique parts of each experience. This helps us accept whatever comes our way.

Seeing the world through the eyes of a child also helps us be present and in the moment. By being present, we open ourselves to the newness of any experience or interaction rather than letting our expectations limit us.

Finally, and most importantly, we need to focus on appreciation instead of expectation. By looking for things to appreciate rather than for the things that didn't go our way, we can avoid or release those feelings of disappointment, anger, and resentment. That's not to say that eliminating expectation is easy, because it isn't. We have expectations around everything from how our positive performance at work should or will be acknowledged to how our family and friends might celebrate our birthday or even how our partner should take over clean-up duties after we've cooked a gourmet meal. And most of the time, we don't even realize we have these expectations until they aren't met and we are hit with disappointment, anger, or resentment. When that upset hits us, we need to take a moment to refocus on our appreciation. We can appreciate ourselves for having done a great job or overdelivering for a client. We can appreciate that we are able to celebrate with people who are important to us. We can appreciate that we were able to share a tasty meal with someone we care about. By shifting our focus onto the positives, we can move from being angry to being grateful.

What does this all mean in terms of sharing our stories? Well, when we share our stories, we aim to do so without the expectation of a specific reaction. Instead, we can simply appreciate those who take the time to listen. By doing this, we open up the possibility for those listeners to hear exactly what they need to hear in that moment, even if it isn't what you expected them to take away. And you may be surprised how impactful that can be.

# The Importance of Gratitude

A few years ago, I found myself at a point of overwhelm, as I have been at several points in my life. My work, while plentiful, wasn't fulfilling; I wasn't growing or being challenged. My father had been diagnosed with terminal cancer, and my siblings and I were managing his care the best we could while navigating our own careers and family schedules and all the other things life threw at us. I felt a need to get my life in order: to be a better friend, a better sister, a better daughter, a better aunt, a better me. I was filling my lists with all the things I thought I should do in order to be successful—but whose definition of success was I trying to fulfill?

The truth is that I was trying to be everything for everyone. And let's face it, none of us can achieve that.

One day, at a time when I didn't know what else to do, the opportunity to take a course crossed my path. It was led by the very successful Arianna Huffington, co-founder of the Huffington Post as well as founder and CEO of Thrive Global, and it was based on a book she had written called *Thrive*. And that's exactly what I wanted: to thrive in the midst of whatever situation I found myself.

In both the book and the course, Huffington talks about our tendency to discount the importance of sleep and how we can accomplish more if we sleep more (she later published a book solely on this topic). She also covered topics like meditating, exercising, being selective about the people and projects to whom we give our time, and taking a break from our devices. However, the part that had the biggest impact on me was the part about gratitude.

There has been a lot of talk about gratitude since I took that course, so maybe you think you've heard it all by now. But in case you haven't, research has proven that intentional gratitude lowers stress, promotes better sleep, increases kindness and compassion, creates a greater sense of calm, and even strengthens our immune systems. As a result, many of us have tried all kinds of methods to bring more gratitude into our lives, from keeping journals to working on being more present in the moment—taking time to smell the roses, so to speak.

We don't doubt the power of gratitude because it's one of the first lessons we learn in life. We learn to say please and thank you when we first start to speak. Our parents remind us to be grateful throughout our childhood and into our teenage years, often to the point of frustration on both sides. We even have specific times of year—holidays, birthdays, anniversaries—that are about acknowledging our blessings, exchanging gifts, gathering together, and celebrating.

But what about when we are alone? When there is nothing to celebrate? When we experience something devastating? How do we find gratitude then?

In the book and course, Huffington gives a few examples of exercises she adopted in her own life to ensure she remembered to practice gratitude every day. One option she mentions is the ten-finger gratitude exercise, first suggested by clinical psychologist Mark Williams, where once a day you list ten things you're grateful for and count them out on your fingers. While finding ten things may be challenging, that's the point of the exercise: to bring into awareness the tiny, previously unnoticed elements of your day.

However, the exercise that stuck with me was finding an account-ability partner with whom I could share three things I was grateful for at the end of each day. When I mentioned what I'd been learning to one of my friends, she offered to be someone I could do this with.

So, for all those days and weeks and months in the midst of my father's decline in health and eventual passing, this friend and I would text each evening just to share the three things we took a moment to notice in our days. Some weeks the same things showed up time after time: sunrises, sunsets, the unconditional love and comfort given to us by our respective dogs. And even as I was sitting by my father's bed in the hospice as we waited for him to take his final breath, this practice made me find the good in every day: the laughter as I shared memories with my siblings, the wonderful friends and extended family who visited or provided meals for us, the morning coffee with Baileys shared with a family down the hall, the care and love and respect we received from the staff at the hospice after his passing. Even today, as I think back to that time more than six years ago now, the gratitude and blessings almost overwhelm me—they definitely overshadow the sadness and devastation of those days.

My friend and I fell out of this practice early into the following year—life gets busy and priorities change. But we kept it up when I needed it most, which is something else to be grateful for.

These days, our world is filled with so much hatred, fear, and strife. We hear about wars and shootings on a daily basis. About refugees fleeing for their lives. About hunger and disease and natural disasters all over the world. There's a lot to feel hopeless about, which is why we need to practice gratitude even more. We need hope. We need light. We need to find the good in every day.

Practicing gratitude is even more important when it comes to healing our stories. When we can find things to be thankful for in the most challenging of times, we discover the positives that these experiences have brought to us—things like revealing our strength or helping us find the good that has come about because of those difficulties.

Tony Robbins—a well-known author, coach, speaker, and philanthropist—often says, "What if life were happening for us rather than to us? If you can take your worst day and find something to turn it into your best day, then you find grace and gratitude. And life is always a gift."

When I started to look at my life from this perspective—that everything was happening for me rather than to me—the way I saw every part of my story changed. Instead of seeing myself as a victim of my circumstances, I started looking for the lesson, the blessing, the gift in each and every situation. That gift is definitely not always immediately apparent, and it's easier to find with some experiences than others, but it's always there.

# Help, I Need Somebody

I would be remiss if I ended this section on healing without addressing that sometimes, we need to bring in a professional to facilitate deeper healing. It's natural for us to go to experts like personal trainers or tennis coaches when we need help with getting in shape or fixing our serve. We even hire business coaches when we are looking to develop management or leadership skills. So why wouldn't we seek out professional help when we have grief, trauma, or another personal challenge holding us back from living a fulfilling life?

I saw my first therapist, a psychiatrist, at the age of twelve, after my parents had discovered my problem with binge eating. It wasn't a comfortable situation; in fact, I was mortified that there was something so wrong with me that I needed to see a shrink.

I admit that my twelve-year-old perception might have been just a little skewed due to how psychiatrists were portrayed in movies and television at that time. Counselling or therapy wasn't as common or accepted as it is today; it actually carried a lot of stigma. The words I most often associated with therapy were "crazy," "sick," and "medicated." There was this overall impression that instead of discussing our internal problems, we should keep quiet and sweep these feelings under the rug. Thankfully, these days we know better. But even outside of those beliefs, just the idea that I needed such extreme help made me feel like my parents thought I was, in fact, crazy—or at the very least, that I was weak.

It wasn't until I was eighteen or nineteen that I started to open up to the idea of counselling or therapy. I was even pursuing a degree in psychology because I was fascinated by the way the mind worked and why we do the things we do. During this phase of my life, a mentor told me that she believed everyone could benefit from a year of therapy, no matter what their life looked like. She went on to say that there's no better opportunity to talk about yourself, your thoughts, your dreams, your fears, your challenges, anything you were feeling or facing in that moment.

In particular, though, there are times when we need a trained professional to help us process certain life experiences. While a friend or family member can be a great listener, they don't have the specialized training to guide you through all the mental and emotional impacts of trauma, stress, or even unhealthy behaviours. A trained professional also provides us with confidentiality, objectivity, and yes, undivided attention.

Perhaps the most important benefit is that a trained professional isn't going to try to provide a quick fix the way many of our loved ones will out of their desire for us to be happy. A therapist's job is to encourage open and honest dialogue to help us identify and understand how various events, experiences, and other stresses impact our lives and overall well-being. They help us discover and deal with the root causes of the challenges we've been facing, and then they help us develop strategies to manage or overcome them. They help us better understand ourselves, creating room for growth and healing.

When looking for a counsellor or therapist, it is important to find someone who is a good fit for you and your specific needs. You wouldn't hire a plumber to do an electrical job or a tennis coach to teach you how to surf, would you? In the same way, a business coach or a life coach is most likely not going to be the right person to help you heal grief, trauma, or relationship issues. Finding the right fit means finding someone who you can trust, who you feel comfortable having these difficult conversations with, and who is able and prepared to work with your specific needs and issues.

Since that initial experience with the psychiatrist, I've not only grown more comfortable with the idea of therapy, but I've also embraced it in more than one period of my life. I've seen several different counsellors over the years for a variety of reasons: to assist me through seasons of grief and loss, to help me deal with my early life trauma, and more recently, to address some triggers that were holding me back.

Regardless of how we approach our personal challenges, whether it's on our own or with professional help, we must do what it takes to put ourselves on the path to healing. We must acknowledge our judgments and release our expectations, both of ourselves and of others. We must let go of the need to be perfect and practice gratitude in our daily lives. We must address our hurts so that we do not continue to hurt others. And once we have done this, we are ready to share our stories in a way that will benefit those who listen.

That being said, you don't *have* to share this growth and transformation with anyone, as much as I encourage you to. In the end, just going through this healing process yourself will change the direction of your life, because you will have changed how you see your struggles. You will have changed how you view the other people involved in your situation. You will have changed how you feel about yourself. And you will have changed how you approach the future.

# Telling Your Story

✳

*"Share your story with someone. You never know how one sentence of your life story could inspire someone to rewrite their own."*

— *Demi Lovato*

# Providing Hope

Once we've done the work of diving into our stories to heal all the hurt and difficult emotions surrounding them, we have been transformed. We have taken our experiences from burden to blessing, from tragedy to triumph, and even relabeled ourselves from victim to victor. And this is when it is beneficial to share what we've been through—all of it. Because now, we can provide hope.

Have you ever experienced a few days of grey weather? Here in Vancouver, BC, our winters have a lot of them. As I am writing this, the past couple of months have seen weeks of heavy rain and dark skies. Times like this can sap your energy, making it difficult to get anything accomplished. You want to curl up with a good book and a hot drink in front of a fireplace rather than doing anything productive.

But then, you get a day with blue skies and bright sunshine, and everything changes. Everyone becomes lighter and happier. The parks and trails are filled with people enjoying the sunshine and fresh air, even if it's cold. You feel like you can conquer anything.

Why is it that our moods, outlooks, and even energy levels can be changed by something as seemingly minor as the weather? We still have to cook meals. We still have to do our errands and laundry. We still have to go work. But everything feels different because the sunshine, the positivity, the lightness and brightness all bring hope.

The same thing happens when we share our stories. Talking about the dark times, the challenging times, and the heartbreaking times can be difficult and emotional. But when we do share these stories, it's usually because we've made it through to the other side. We have survived. We have conquered. We have recognized our own strength and resilience. We've learned something about ourselves, our skills, and our capacity for doing the hard work it takes to overcome these events. And there's always someone out there who is caught up in their own dark, challenging, or heartbreaking times who needs to know that you made it through—that there will be bright sunshine at the end of the dark days. They desperately need hope that they, too, can make it, just like you did.

This is why we *must* share our stories—and not just the difficult ones, but also the triumphant ones. The ones where we achieve our goals. The ones where we are living our dreams.

Sometimes, finding the stories that can provide hope requires looking in unexpected places. One example comes from Deborah, one of the co-authors of the collaborative book *The Gift in Your Story*. She was convinced that she didn't have a story worth sharing, but she still participated in all the workshops and programs with the other potential authors. One by one, we discussed potential life events or stories that she could dive into. She could talk about her mother's battle with cancer and being there for those crucial last days of her life, or she could share about abandoning her hope of following her long-held dream career, or even about making the very difficult decision to sell the family home where four generations had lived. None of them seemed right. Why? Mainly because she hadn't yet found the "gift" in each of these situations. Each one still brought up a series of difficult emotions, and she just wasn't ready to share them yet.

Then, one session, she talked about how she often "mothered" the young people she worked with over the years, and her story started to make itself known. You see, Deborah had always wanted to have children and had gone through the IVF process more than once with no success. It was hugely disappointing. She and her husband had since done their grieving and moved on to have successful careers and busy, fulfilled lives. But what she connected with in this moment was that she wasn't without a family of her own because she created that family wherever she went, particularly in her work environments. She brought people into her life and home and cared for them in so many little—and big—ways. She ensured that the young men she worked with in a home goods warehouse had good, healthy meals at least once a week, and she celebrated all their big life events. She invited friends for holiday meals when they had nowhere else to go. She and her husband even opened their home to young people who needed a place to stay for a few nights or longer. They embraced anyone who needed some love and care and, yes, family.

While Deborah's journey to becoming a mother wasn't successful by the traditional definition, she still found a way to create a family and now refers regularly to her "kids" of all ages and from all walks of life. And that message of finding success in non-traditional ways can provide hope to many people facing similar struggles.

Our stories provide hope that tomorrow will be just a little easier or a little brighter. Hope that there is something positive waiting for us on the other side. Hope that maybe, just maybe, the sun will come out tomorrow.

# Not Boring Either

When I talk about my belief that everyone's story is worth sharing, most people respond that their story is too boring to have an impact on anyone. Maybe that's what you think too.

I totally get why you might feel this way. Let's face it, the stories we remember the most are the ones of incredible success or devastating loss, or even a combination of both. And it's true that not everyone has a story like mine. How many people do you know who were orphaned as a toddler? Or who had a family member suffer a devastating stroke, locking them inside her body for more than sixteen years now? That being said, I am not the first to be orphaned, nor will I be the last, and people have strokes every day. So, perhaps my story isn't so unique after all.

We all have times when we feel our story is just average and that nobody would care to hear it, myself included. A big reason for this is that we have lived with ourselves our whole lives. I know that sounds silly—of course we have! But when we experience something for days, weeks, months, sometimes years on end, it stops being remarkable or unusual. It's just who we are, or what our life looks like, or what we are working to achieve.

Basically, the more we do something, the more we imprint it on our experience and the more "normal" or "boring" it becomes—to us. But it isn't normal to everyone else, and that is an important distinction to make.

You have something special—or more likely, several things—that make you and your story unique. Even siblings growing up under the same roof will have different experiences because we all process things through our own lens. My sister and I were both orphaned and then adopted into the same family, but the way we remember and experience these things and their effects on us are and will always be vastly different because we think and feel and process things in a completely unique way.

Consider anyone who has been affected by a huge tragedy. Every single person who was in the towers at the World Trade Center on 9/11 experienced the same horrific event, yet they will all have incredibly unique stories. Where in the buildings were they? What was their route out? What were they thinking/feeling/experiencing? And what about their loved ones, hearing the news and trying to get in touch with them?

We could hear one hundred stories from this single event, and they would all be different. Each person's experience is unique; so are their post-event struggles and the ways they have grown and changed because of their experience.

I chose this example because we are all aware of it. Why do people still remember where they were when the planes hit the World Trade Center? Because it has had—or continues to have—an effect on us. We are connected to it by whatever emotion or mix of emotions it brings up in us. Sadness for the lives lost. Frustration or anger at whatever system we believe failed to prevent the tragedy. Encouraged by the way people helped each other. Inspired by the actions of first responders or passersby. We may even feel motivated to take action ourselves because of the people speaking out and calling for change.

When we connect with an emotion—any emotion—we move

from feeling isolated and alone to feeling connected and validated. We stop feeling alone in our grief or anger or any combination of emotions, and we become part of a larger community. We find belonging.

This is why sharing our stories is important, no matter how "boring" we think they are. In addition to remembering exceptional stories, we also remember those stories that connect with something in our own lives: our feelings or emotions, a period of our lives, a struggle we've had with our kids or parents or friends, anything that resonates with us at that very moment.

Your story isn't boring if it doesn't involve tragedy, incredible achievement, or any other kind of low or high. Why? Because somebody somewhere needs to hear it, connect with it, and take something from it.

You may say, "But I grew up with such a boring, normal life. We didn't want for anything, my parents stayed together and are still married, we lived in a great neighbourhood, went to good schools, could afford vacations during holidays…" whatever your definition of "normal" or "middle class" or "the same as most of the people I know" may be. But remember what I said about how we've lived with ourselves for our whole lives? We need to look at our lives from an outsider's perspective in order to see the things that will stand out to someone else. And I would venture to guess that anyone who really knows you would be able to list several things that make your story unique and valuable. Let me ask you a few questions:

- Have you ever felt a strong emotion? Inconsolable grief, sadness, or pain? Indescribable anger? Extreme elation?

- Have you ever failed at anything? An exam? A class? A goal?

- How about *feeling* as though you've failed at something? Parenting? Managing your finances? Disappointing your parents, your significant other, your children, yourself?

- Have you ever faced a difficult challenge and come through the other side feeling as though you've learned something? Perhaps grown as a person? Felt a sense of achievement?

- Have you ever stepped out of your comfort zone to try something new, possibly something that scared you, and succeeded? Perhaps playing a new sport, dancing in public, or moving to a new city? Or maybe you didn't feel successful at whatever it was. Did you learn something about yourself in the process?

If you answered "yes" to any of these questions, then you have a story. If any memory or person or idea popped into your mind as you read these questions, then you have a story. If any emotion came up for you, even if it didn't have a specific memory attached to it, then you have a story.

When we feel emotion, it is a signal that something is going on for us. It tells us that there is something important in the experiences associated with that emotion—something that taught us a lesson, helped us grow, or perhaps is still waiting for us to figure it out.

The only way to find the bigger piece that gives the story meaning and purpose is to take the time to look for it. Don't just focus on what you went through or struggled with; that might be a part of it, but it's not the full story. Instead, the lasting learning piece can be found in the way the experience changed you. Maybe it changed your views on something, opened your eyes to a bigger truth, or helped you overcome something that had been holding you back. When you find these areas of growth or realize a truth, you have found what someone else—or perhaps several others—might need to hear.

# Facing the Roadblocks

Telling our story—or, more correctly, finding the right story to tell—can be overwhelming. I personally struggled with this for more than ten years. After I realized that even a small part of my story could inspire someone else, like the couple at lunch who were inspired by my commitment to focus on my health for six weeks, I knew I had to share it. If even one person could feel less alone by hearing my story, then I needed to put it out there. However, I didn't know what "out there" meant, and I definitely didn't know how to do it.

The most difficult aspect of this was figuring out where to start. I always felt that my story was overwhelming, and that it sounded too unbelievable—like the main character in a very dramatic soap opera. I honestly wondered if anyone would believe me.

Also, there were so many different parts and people involved that it got confusing. My mom—my birth mom, not my adoptive mom. Or my grandmother—my adoptive father's mother as compared to my adoptive mother's mother, or the mother of either of my birth parents. And don't forget the siblings and aunts and uncles (with both sets of parents too!) and, and, and… Whew! You can understand why I found it so overwhelming.

You see, I always thought that sharing my story involved going through everything that had happened since I was born, chronologically detailing my life. However, the word "memoir" (the category most often associated with biographies or telling our own stories) comes from the word memory, and our memories don't work chronologically. We remember bits and pieces as they relate to what's going on in our lives or because we are purposefully thinking about a specific topic or lesson.

It is the same with sharing our stories. Recognizing that I didn't have to tell my whole story was freeing. When I focused on just one single piece of my story—what happened, how I felt, how I struggled, and then how it turned around or what I learned from it—I discovered that nobody needed to know everything that led up to that experience. The part I shared was enough to be inspirational and encouraging all on its own.

And this is where we can all start: with sharing any memory we want. Take that memory and tie it together with something it taught you and why that's important to you. What did you learn? How did that event shape who you are or your values? How did you grow or change?

Whatever your reasons are for sharing your story, take the time to honour your own experience. Don't think about who might want to hear or read it—maybe no one ever will. But if someone does, they will appreciate hearing what matters to you, not what you think they want to hear.

One example of this comes from some siblings I know who found stacks of letters after the death of the family matriarch. These were letters between her and her pen pal from another country to whom she had been writing for over fifty years—since before the second world war. The family had these letters published into a book and distributed among all her relatives. Reading it not only showed this woman's grandchildren and great-grandchildren what the world, and her own life, was like during the war, but it also gave each family member a glimpse into who their mother, aunt, grandmother, or great-grandmother was outside of those defined roles. She wasn't thinking about how her relatives might feel or what she was sharing as she wrote these letters; she was pouring her heart and her life out to a wonderful friend, who was doing the same thing right back. That collection is a real treasure to all her descendants.

Another roadblock that prevents us from telling our stories, especially ones that include our family or friends, is the fear of offending or upsetting someone. Our anxiety over the fact that we may not be painting a parent, sibling, friend, former boss, whomever it might be in the most favourable light can stop us in our tracks.

I was worried for a very long time that parts of my story would upset my family. My experiences were all being shared from my own perspective, and I knew that I wouldn't always be able to paint others in the best light. So, I held back and kept quiet for a long time.

But then I discovered something that changed everything for me. Through conversations with my sister, my other siblings, and even my therapist, I started to understand that even though my sister went through the same fire as I did, even though we both lost our parents, and even though she was adopted into the same family I was, her story was not the same as mine. She felt different things, she had different struggles, our entire experiences were different, even though they seemed identical from the outside. In addition, I realized that I wasn't telling her story, nor did I need to do so. I was simply telling my own.

This lesson is important for all of us. We have to remember that our stories are uniquely our own. Difficult experiences happen to all of us, and not one of us is perfect—as a parent, as a child, as a sibling, or as a friend. We make mistakes. We say and do things we later regret. But the people and experiences we find challenging shape who we are and often become our greatest teachers, leading us to understand something new about ourselves or find a strength we didn't know we possessed.

When telling stories like this, the key is to do so without blame, without putting someone else in the role of being the antagonist or bully, and without assuming what they might feel, think, or believe. And that's not an easy task if we haven't done the deeper work of healing ourselves.

Finally, we need to believe that our story is worth telling. Whatever your story, there's a reason it's working its way to the surface, nudging you from time to time. It's often because you haven't found anything like it out there in the libraries or bookstores. It's a story you would love to read.

Imagine if everybody believed that their story was boring or not worth sharing. In that world, we wouldn't have many of the great books, movies, songs, and television shows that we all love because someone's worry and self-doubt would have stopped them from putting pen to paper in the first place. But don't just take my word for it. Here are some examples of how others have been inspired or affected by other people's stories:

"All my life, my mother told me every person has one good story to tell, a story no one else on the planet can tell—the story of his or her own life. She implored me to tell my story while I could, explaining what a disappointment it was that she had never gotten around to telling *her* story." —S. G. R.

"I feel I have learned something from every personal story I have heard or read. Stories from those I admire have helped shape me to who I am today and guided my decisions and life choices. Stories of those who have suffered have made me more compassionate, have helped me to see the world through a different lens, and have driven me to try and act in ways to avoid further suffering (mine and beyond). Each story acts as a reference point and, whether I am aware of it or not, has likely impacted me in some way." —*D. S.*

"When I read and heard Jamie Kern Lima say 'My past mistakes or miscalculations would not determine who I'll become,' I realized that it didn't matter that I didn't know the 'how' to raising my girls in one home with only one mom and only one dad. It was like removing a cloak of darkness that I felt like I had to carry for the rest of my life. I felt like I had regained the confidence to let go and move onward and upward!" —*N. G.*

"I shared my story in *The Gift in Your Story*. A family member read it and then told me that they never really understood me and all my moving around the world, but now, because of reading my chapter, they were really impressed with the decisions I had made and understood me so much better." —*T.L.*

No matter who you are or what you have experienced (or have not experienced), your story matters, and it is worth sharing. And if you don't start telling your own story, nobody else will.

# Getting Started

Once we've recognized that we do have a valuable story to share, one of the hardest things to decide is how or where we should start. When we don't know where to begin, it's hard to decide where we should focus or even where we want to end up.

The problem is that we waste so much time and energy trying to figure out the so-called right way to tell our story that we never start at all. I'm guilty of this myself. Way back when I decided that my story did have worth and needed to be shared, I got stuck on trying to figure out the how. I didn't think I was a writer, a public speaker, a performer—there were so many things I decided I was *not*, which left me with very few options. And because I couldn't figure that part out, I kept putting it on the proverbial back burner and letting the rest of life take precedence.

But the truth that our stories—*all* our stories—are important kept showing up. It was everywhere: in my events, in my conversations, in the media I chose to consume.

So, I just started writing whatever was on my mind on any given day. A person, a memory, random thoughts. I did that for several months and ended up with eighty type-written pages. I gave those pages to a few people to read, and the responses varied. One person commented that she liked my style of writing. Another wanted more, wanted to know what happened next. And the third said she just felt a lot of pain in my writing, which was when I knew I wasn't ready to fully share my story yet. I didn't want my readers, or anyone hearing my story, to feel pain or discomfort or even, as I've mentioned more than once, pity.

I put my writing aside as I continued to try and figure out just *how* to tell my story—or even part of my story—without the hurt, pain, anger, and sadness. I focused on my work, and eventually I began to see how stories fit into my event planning business. How all along I'd been helping my clients—mostly charities or groups raising money—tell their stories in a way that made the listener want to take action, be part of the solution, or do something differently. It wasn't so much about the charity or the organization, but rather the end result. What did they want their guests, listeners, sponsors, and donors to do? How did they want them to feel?

It's the same with my story, and with your stories. We have to consider not just our experience, but also the end result we want from sharing our stories. Do we want our audience to walk away feeling the difficult emotions? Do we want them to feel inspired into taking action? What do we want the takeaway to be?

That takeaway is the gift that our stories provide. Once we have discovered that gift, then we can pass it on to others, and they can be inspired to take their own action.

That was my own long way around figuring out which stories to tell and which stories needed more inside work and healing first. But how do we find those stories in the first place?

To start, we can begin with a simple phrase: "My life changed when..." This phrase may not seem like much, but it opens up a world of possibilities when it comes to discovering our stories, especially the important ones. We can all find multiple instances when our lives shifted direction, and they all centre on a turning point that has a story behind it. For instance, a few events that come to mind for me to finish this prompt include:

- When my parents died in a fire.

- When I thought about taking my own life.

- When I realized I was burned out.

Each one of these is the start to a story. Something I learned. Something I discovered. Something I overcame.

This is one starting point, but not the only one. Sometimes, the easiest way to dive into our stories is to remember the people and events that played a major role in our lives—family traditions, birthday parties, special dinners. Who was around the table at those events? Where and when did a particular tradition start?

You may also think about how you spent your days as a child. Favourite activities? Things you could do for hours and feel like just moments had passed? Some treasured items that belonged to a grandparent? Something you loved about your first pet? The list goes on and on.

In August, 2021, I was exploring my own stories with the goal of sharing one every day. I called it the Nature and Nurture Project— partly because I was in a unique position of having grown up knowing and interacting with some of my birth family as well as my adoptive family, and partly because I had some specific stories from both sides that I wanted to share.

In truth, this project really started out as a way to remember some of the people, moments, and experiences that are still important to me today. It was fun to reflect on the significant people in my life—particularly the significant adults from my childhood—and the different ways in which who they were at their core had a profound effect on who I have become: my likes and dislikes, my favourite hobbies and pastimes, and even my chosen career path.

I certainly didn't have thirty-one stories planned out ahead of time. I knew I wanted to share about my adoptive father, Bruce—how he was the first human to ride a famous wooden rollercoaster, and how much he continued to love rollercoasters throughout his life. I wanted to talk about his love for horses and horse racing and how that started with his uncle, who was a successful jockey. I also wanted to tell the story of my grandfather and his generous spirit.

However, the days where I had no idea what story I was going to tell often ended up being the days I found and shared some of my favourite memories. These stories were sparked by anything from items that I'd secured away in storage to the story I'd written the day before. You see, the more we dive into our stories—particularly the ones that had some role in shaping who we are—the more stories we discover. One memory spurs another.

Even going through old photos helps spark our stories. Each one comes with a memory or a different way of seeing things now that we have the perspective of time and wisdom. Would I have an enormous love for music without the musical ability of and stories from my grandparents? What about their desire for my siblings and I to learn to play an instrument, so much so that they even purchased our family piano? Or the way they would patiently sit through our (sometimes horrible) family recitals? Maybe I would still love music as much as I do now, but maybe not.

Every holiday, every celebration, every family tradition is a memory ripe with stories. Stories of traditions we kept as we created homes and families of our own. Stories of accidents and mishaps, like the time my grandmother caught on fire while carrying the flaming Christmas pudding. (Don't worry, she wasn't injured, just surprised.) Each one of these memories is an opportunity to revisit an important part of our lives, both the good and the bad. It's a chance to see who we were, all we've learned, and how far we've come.

I bet if you think about it, you have several stories that relate solely to your family traditions alone. For me, I remember how my siblings and I used to get so excited about decorating the Christmas tree. We made ornaments in school every year, something out of a clay or paper that likely ripped or fell apart on the way home. You know the kind. We would wait, perhaps not so patiently, for our parents to let us decorate and add our new creations to the tree. Dinner had to be cleaned up first, and then they would put the lights on—often a painstakingly long operation as our parents tried to ensure they were evenly spaced. But then, finally, it was our turn. My siblings and I carefully (or maybe haphazardly) placed our favourite decorations on the tree—the ones we'd made, the paper chains we had created with our friends, and other sturdy ornaments. The delicate ones were reserved for more careful hands.

And then, the tinsel—those magical, shiny strands that had a mind of their own. We'd start out with one or two pieces at a time and quickly progressed to throwing handfuls at the tree. By the time we kids were finished, the bottom half of the tree was covered in clumps of tinsel while the top of the tree was rather bare.

When we awoke in the morning, though, the tree looked a lot

different. Gone were the clumps of tinsel and most of the handmade decorations. After we had gone to bed, our parents had cleaned the mess and reorganized all the decorations, making sure to keep the most fragile ones higher up where they would be safe from accidental bumps.

The more we revisit our stories, the more we discover new information, new lessons, new insights into why we are the way we are. And any one of these things can be your starting point for choosing a story that will impact others.

# Embrace Vulnerability

Sharing our stories in a meaningful, transformative way isn't easy. On the plus side, we can remember so many wonderful people and events that taught us something new and exciting about the world around us and our place in it. The other side, the more difficult one, is that it means revisiting some of the worst times of our lives and often experiencing the uncomfortable emotions that come with them.

That's where embracing our vulnerability comes in: facing, feeling, and yes, even talking about the anger, fear, sadness, loneliness, or whatever emotion comes up for you. Doing this is scary, but it can be so worth it.

One of the best parts of the human experience is the ability to truly connect with others. Our lives are set up for it: we are raised in families, we often work in groups, we love in pairs (or more), and we truly thrive in friendships. It's why we historically gathered in tribes—we need connection in order to survive. Research suggests that satisfying, intimate relationships—either romantic or platonic—are a fundamental part of finding happiness, meaning, and purpose in our lives. Yet in today's world, we are seeing more and more disconnection, which leads to loneliness, depression, and broken relationships.

So, how do we open ourselves to true connection? Well, we have to let go of who we think we should be and allow our true selves to be known. Essentially, we have to be vulnerable.

Brené Brown—a professor, author, speaker, and podcast host specializing in vulnerability and shame—defines vulnerability as "uncertainty, risk, and emotional exposure." She also describes it as "the willingness to say 'I love you' first, the willingness to invest in a relationship that may or may not work out, and the willingness to do something when there are no guarantees." These actions can be quite uncomfortable and scary, but we have to open ourselves up to this discomfort; otherwise, we limit our ability to fully experience fundamental parts of life such as creativity, love, trust, joy, and belonging.

The biggest problem with vulnerability is that we see it as being courageous and daring in others, yet we see it as weakness in our own lives. Being vulnerable involves showing emotion, and many of us have been taught to keep the more uncomfortable emotions to ourselves. Why? Because those emotions not only make us uncomfortable, but also often make others feel the same way. So, to combat those feelings of weakness, we put on a mask of "having it all together." We pretend we don't need help, we aren't afraid of anything, and we don't make mistakes.

Sounds a little like perfectionism, doesn't it?

I battle this tendency all the time. It's tough to admit when things aren't going well, and the best way to overcome this is to learn to embrace vulnerability. Doing so not only helps us improve our connections with others, but it also increases our self-confidence and self-worth, builds trust, and promotes belonging and acceptance.

This is where our stories come in. We need to see and share them without fear of shame, and without fear of our emotions being brought to the surface and possibly even spilling over. We need to share the truth of our experiences, because that is where our most important lessons are found.

Part of being vulnerable is acknowledging that your experience is unique to you. Just because someone else didn't (or won't) experience a challenge or event the same way you did does not make your (or their) experience wrong or unimportant. No two people will experience an event in the same way, nor will they tell their story in the same way. To better understand this, consider this parable of the blind men and the elephant:

*Once upon a time, there was a village that was completely inhabited by blind people. One day, an elephant came to the village. Since none of the people had ever seen an elephant before, they all gathered around the animal to figure out how it looked.*

*The man who touched the trunk said, "An elephant is like a thick tree branch."*

*"No! It's like a pillar," said another who touched the leg.*

*"You're both wrong!" said a third who touched the tail. "The elephant is like a rope."*

*"Oh no!" shouted another who was feeling the belly. "It's like a wall"*

*And a man who was touching the tusk said, "Come on, guys! The elephant is nothing but a solid pipe."*

*They began arguing and fighting, each of them insisting he was right. They were getting agitated and frustrated with each other.*

*A wise man was passing by the village when he heard the men shouting. He stopped and asked, "What's the matter?"*

*The blind men told him that they could not agree about what an elephant was, and each told him what he thought it looked like.*

*The wise man smiled and said, "All of you are right. But because each one of you touched a different part of the elephant, you all had different images of what an elephant looked like. And just because each one of you imagined an elephant through his own experience doesn't mean that the other person's image of the elephant is wrong. An elephant has all the features that you described and much more. But you can never tell what an elephant is by just touching one part of it."*

Let's not forget that each of us is looking at a different version of reality; a small aspect of life that's coloured with our own perceptions and experiences. We are all touching just one part of the elephant, and by sharing our stories, we can create a complete picture that helps us feel not quite so alone and often gives us new insight into our own knowledge and healing.

It's easy to hide our vulnerability—to keep those deep, emotional, and sometimes dark parts of ourselves hidden and locked away. We put on that mask and hide or make light of our pain, our fear, our failures, or our weaknesses. And we do it because vulnerability is scary.

Taking off that mask and letting others know that you aren't feeling confident or happy or even sure about who you are or where you are in life is never easy. However, vulnerability is necessary for growth. When we embrace our vulnerability by being honest about our stories and all we have learned, we allow our imperfections to be seen. And when we accept and share our own imperfections, we more easily accept that others are also imperfect. We can move beyond our tendency to judge and criticize, and we can then connect more easily with others.

I'm not saying that being vulnerable is easy—in fact, it requires incredible strength and courage. And you also don't have to offer every detail of your life or trauma up to every person; you can pick and choose who you are vulnerable with and how vulnerable you want to be. Before sharing your story, consider your audience: is it your family? A close friend? A group of strangers? What do you want them to understand after hearing your story? The answer to that last question will help guide your decision of how much you should share.

When we *do* find the right opportunity to be vulnerable, we can then fully embrace the human experience. Because when we can be open and honest about our stories—about the good, the bad, and the ugly—we make it safe for others to do the same. And that is where we find authentic connection.

# Share Your Story the Right Way

I've spent several years talking about why our stories are so important. I've spoken about why we need to revisit them, heal them, and then share them so that others don't feel alone in their own struggles and challenges—so they know there is someone else out there who has made it through. And hopefully, the people who hear our stories will then be inspired to do the work, to keep going, to heal their own hearts and experiences and lives. And as more and more people heal themselves, we contribute to the bigger healing of our world. And yes, that is what our stories can do.

And yet.

There is an issue arising within our current culture. I am not the only person talking about how now is the time to share our stories. Every coach, every online guru, every influencer, every inspirational or motivational speaker in every realm. And often, we are being told to put these stories on our social media channels.

This is where we need to practice a little more restraint, because social media is not necessarily the place to share every story or lesson. Public forums like Facebook and TikTok are a great place for us to talk about some life or business truth we realized while exercising, or about trying to learn something new, or about participating in a competition of some kind. Those stories are not what I'm concerned about.

More and more frequently, it seems, people are sharing their deeper stories on these platforms. The ones that involve trauma.

The ones that involve tragedy. The ones that cause deep emotional, physical, mental, even spiritual pain. Abuse. Rape. Illness. Accidents. Death. So many people are trying to make an impact, trying to be seen and heard, trying to get followers or views or clients, that these stories are being thrown out into the world in thirty to sixty second sound bites. They might come as a text-based post on Facebook, as some photos and a description on Instagram, or as a response to a TikTok challenge or trend.

If we are truly honest with ourselves, putting these stories out into the world like this isn't about helping anyone else. We're focused on being seen as someone who is strong, someone who is resilient, someone who has overcome. We aren't thinking about how these stories might affect anyone who is coming across them, and that's a problem, because these bite-sized glimpses into our bigger stories can have an unintended effect.

The worst-case scenario is like the aftermath of a drive-by shooting. An innocent bystander is scrolling through their social media feed or watching one reel after another, and they are unintentionally hit by one of these huge, traumatic revelations that bring up something from their past—something they have not dealt with and are not ready to do so.

In simpler terms, these posts are triggers that can open the door to all kinds of traumatic stress for the person who comes across them. Some people have their own stories that they have been trying to deal with, figure out, heal from—or worse, their own current experiences that they are avoiding—and seeing your thirty-second revelation while scrolling social media is like setting off a bomb in their life. It can trigger memories and nightmares and panic attacks and all other kinds of post-traumatic stress responses.

Sharing these stories on social media is especially problematic if you haven't done the work to heal from those events or don't have the opportunity to talk about the healing process. In that case, you have offered all the trauma with none of the hope.

Another important thing to do before telling your story is to ask yourself, "Is this actually my story to tell?" There are times when fully telling our story may necessitate including part of someone else's story, but we need to be careful in doing so. I've mentioned this before; we have to be sure to stick to the facts of how this part of their story had an effect on you and your story. And always, if at all possible, get the other person's permission.

It's not my place to tell my sister's story, or my brother's, mother's, sister-in-law's, or best friend's. I can share verifiable facts of actual things that happened when it is relevant and important to do so, but there is no way I could accurately convey what was truly going on inside them—their feelings, their struggles, the lessons they learned. We all have reasons for sharing or not sharing what has happened in our lives, and we are all in different places on our journeys. Honour that in others as you would hope they would do for you.

Finally, and most importantly, not everyone needs to hear your story, and not everyone *deserves* to hear it.

Your story goes beyond what happened to you. It includes how you reacted to it, how you struggled, how you overcame, how you changed, how you healed, and yes, even the gifts that have come from that entire process. And sharing that story—that deep, life-changing event—deserves, and even *requires*, trust. Trust between you and the audience. Trust that you are going to take each and every listener on that journey with you. Trust that you have created a safe place for the listener so that they won't be triggered in a way that sets a bomb off in their own life.

What's even more crucial, as I mentioned previously, is to take into account how we want our audience to feel. What do we hope to teach them? What do we want them to learn? What action would we like to inspire?

When we share our stories with others, we are entering into a mutual agreement. The audience is giving you their time and attention, and they have made themselves open to wherever your story will take them. In return, you are committing to taking them on a journey, the same journey you travelled. You need to share how it started, the speedbumps you encountered, the difficulties you faced, and how you overcame it all to reach where you are now. Your story needs to include the gift: how you changed, how you grew, how you healed, how you have transformed because of every step of that journey.

When you only share a small snippet of this story, you are doing yourself, and your audience, a disservice. We can't talk about going from a life-changing spinal injury to running a marathon without including the ups and downs we encountered along the way. Well, we *could* do that, but we would be leaving out a significant portion of our journey—the one that really allows us to connect with our audience. The one where they can see themselves and their struggles in the whole story, even if they aren't in the exact same scenario.

We need to be intentional when we choose which story to share and how much of it to reveal. We need to honour both our own journeys and our audience's journeys so that we avoid opening up another's wounds over and over again. And we need to make sure that we're providing hope—that we're showing our audience that they, too, can make it through whatever challenge they're experiencing.

# How to Share Your Story

Once you've picked what story you want to share, the next step is to decide how you want to share it. And for some people, that decision might feel overwhelming. There is a nearly infinite number of ways to share our stories, and in the end, there is no one right answer. How you do it is really up to you and what feels most natural for you.

If you're struggling to decide which direction to take, here are some ideas to get you started. First, you don't have to go public with your story if you don't want to. Perhaps you would rather share with a close friend or two. Perhaps you want to leave something for your family members: your children, grandchildren, and even great-grandchildren. Perhaps you want to create a private journal or blog to capture your thoughts, which you can then share with specific people when you're ready to do so.

If you are ready to share your story in a more public venue, take some time to explore your options and see what feels most natural to you. People most frequently turn to storytelling mediums such as books, blogs, videos, or podcasts, but those aren't your only options. Ask yourself, how do *you* love to express yourself? Are you an artist? A photographer? A writer, a musician, even a dancer or an actor? All of these can be avenues for exploring and sharing your story. There is no right or wrong choice, and what works for someone else might not work for you.

Personally, I have worked to create opportunities for myself and others to share our stories: on my podcast, at The Power of Story

Conference, and through collaborative book projects. In early 2021, we published the first such anthology, titled *The Gift in Your Story*, featuring the stories of eleven amazing women. They all believed they had a story to tell, but how they got there—how they found the right story to share, how they worked through the things that still needed healing, how they found the gift in their stories—was unique. While they all shared in writing for the purposes of this project, some have gone on to find other ways to express their stories: Emily, a painter, has created a series of works that follow her journey and will be publishing a coffee table book featuring her paintings, her process, and her story; Kristin has shared many parts of her stories through her music; and Tammy and Angel have talked about their journeys on my podcast.

We have access to other people's stories every day through theatre, film, television, podcasts, music, dance, paintings, sculpture, and more. Each one of these can capture the emotions of a moment, the struggle, and even the happy or sad conclusion. We all connect with different modes of storytelling, whether we are receiving or sharing. And that's what is important: finding what works for you. The right venue. The right method. The right audience. The method of sharing your story that leaves you feeling empowered and capable. The one where you can fully express yourself, whatever that may look like. There is no one way to do this, so find *your* way.

# What You Can Expect

As we prepare to share our stories, however that might look, it's important to know that telling our stories is *not* easy. In fact, it can be a roller coaster of emotion.

First, there's that slow climb up the steepest hill—making the decision to share your story. This stage involves a deep knowing that you have something important to share with others—something that could help them. Maybe you don't know exactly what that is, or what form it will take, but you want to make a difference in the lives of others. But like the climb up that big first hill of the ride, the closer you get to actually making the decision to go for it, the more your nerves start to take over. You can't quite see what's ahead because you're still facing upwards.

Soon, you reach the peak. You've decided to share your story and you know without a doubt that you can help someone else—possibly many people. And it's exhilarating! But then the fear hits as you start to move forward over that precipice, and your stomach drops. What will people think? What if I hurt the feelings of those closest to me?

Sharing your story—your truth—means being vulnerable. It means opening yourself up to the fact that others may not share your point of view. To others disagreeing with you. To the possibility that your truth, your feelings, your experience of that event might be incredibly different than those of your siblings, your parents, your best friends. And you know what? It will be incredibly different, because no two of us see the same event in the same way. That doesn't make our experience any less valid, or less valuable.

Let's go back to our roller coaster analogy. People react to that first huge drop in different ways. Some scream. Some laugh. Some put their arms up in the air and enjoy the ride. When we decide to share our stories, we will likely feel all these emotions during that first big drop: excitement, fear, doubt, anxiety. And then we get into the rhythm, like the continued climbs and drops of the roller coaster. We build confidence in knowing what's to come, and our fear lessens.

These repeated climbs and drops represent the work of preparing our stories. For writing in particular, this is the needed work of multiple drafts. Of editors helping with sentence structure. Of getting used to seeing our story on the printed page or computer screen. And with time, we start to believe that we sound like an accomplished writer. That we *can* do this.

Once in a while, there might be a surprise. We hit a loop in the middle of the roller coaster, and suddenly we're upside down. Maybe we feel like the editing process is taking some of the raw emotion out of our story, or that we are losing our unique voice. Maybe we discover something new about our journey that has us questioning if we're telling the right story. Or maybe we even get so stuck in wanting it all to be perfect and tied up in a beautiful bow that we always have one more thing we want to add or change. In reality, these things all come down to fear once again. Fear of what others might say, fear of criticism, fear of rejection. The trick is feeling the fear and doing it anyway because you know that someone else needs to hear what you have to say.

Back to our roller coaster analogy. Next is the relief that comes with being at the end of the ride. On the coaster, this is when the rails in front of you start flattening out and the station is in sight. You've made it!

In terms of sharing your story, this is when you near the end of the editing and proofreading process, or whatever other preparations you needed. The hard work is done. You can relax because you have told your story in the best way you know how, and you are able to find your gifts and share them in the process.

But this roller coaster doesn't come to a stop—in fact, it starts picking up speed again, headed into a banked corner you didn't see the first time. The dread, nervousness, and excitement pick back up. This is when you start preparing to release your story to an audience, and to start putting yourself out there publicly. The closer that release date or speaking gig or performance gets, the more those fears and anxieties start to show up. Your start to worry that your story is weak or not impactful or not important. None of this is true. Remember that your story is more interesting than you can ever imagine; you're just too close to it to be able to see the truth.

Now the roller coaster ride is really coming to its end. You pull into the station, and you disembark. You feel elation and achievement, and you're buzzing with energy. This is when your friends and family show up to support you—when they purchase your book or show up to your event and respond with care, positivity, and pride. Why? Because you have been vulnerable. Because you have been honest. And because by sharing your story, you have inspired them with your strength, resilience, and courage.

Yes, it takes courage, incredible courage, to step into that spotlight and say, "This was my experience." But someone out there needs to hear your story, so I urge you to take that step.

We all have a story to share. Are you ready to take the ride?

# Your Story
# May Be
# Your Legacy

*※*

*"If you're going to live, leave a legacy.*
*Make a mark on the world that can't be erased."*

*— Maya Angelou*

# Those Who Came Before

Humans have been able to advance our societies from the hunter-gatherer days because we've learned from our ancestors. We've heard their stories and experiences of discovering the world around them, so we know what crops grow best in each area, what vegetation is safe or poisonous to eat, what animals are a threat to our very being. Every step of our society's progress has been built upon the steps of people who lived and learned through persistence, dedication, research, and even trial and error.

Because of my adoption and my continued relationship with my birth family, I was fortunate to grow up with four sets of grandparents. Of those eight elders, two passed away in my preschool years, before I could form any lasting memories about them. Another when I was twelve or thirteen. I had a few memories of that grandfather, but none of conversations we shared or stories he had to pass on. Two other grandparents (a grandmother and a grandfather) passed in my university years.

It was around the time of these losses that I started to regret missing out on all the stories they never shared, or that I never asked about or listened to. My grandmother who had just passed away was an amazing storyteller, and she would often entertain us all with the misadventures she experienced when travelling, or even at the grocery store. She even wrote out a couple of her experiences and asked me to type them out for her on my brand-new computer so she could submit them to *Reader's Digest* for publishing. But after she was gone, I realized all the things I didn't know—stories about her childhood, her family (who I never met), even moving across the country with my grandfather and two small children to start a new life in a new city.

This is when I had the thought of buying a small handheld tape recorder and having my three surviving grandparents tell me about their lives. I wanted to hear more from my grandmother who often spoke of how horrified her parents were when her new husband moved her to the "wilds of West Vancouver" (now a thriving suburb). I wanted to record the story of my other grandmother, who birthed her third son while her husband was away fighting in World War II. I wanted to hear stories from my grandfather's childhood, which we'd gotten snippets of when his sister would send her yearly letter full of news and old photographs.

I never did it. I never purchased that recorder, and I never asked them to share their stories. It is one of my biggest regrets. Because now they are all gone, as are my adoptive parents, and gone with them are all the stories, all the experiences, all the lessons we could have learned from—lessons that we could have passed on to the next generation.

Not that we are completely without any stories. I spent some time last summer diving into whatever I could remember about my grandparents and my parents that has had a lasting impact on me. Things like my grandparents' love of music and how I developed an appreciation for all kinds of music through them, including swing and big band. Or their generosity, despite their financial circumstances. A love of horses, a passion for shoes (my sister got that one!), even the hobbies they indulged in and the things that brought them joy.

Our stories are an opportunity to pass on knowledge about what we love, what brings us joy, how we struggled, and what we learned. They give us a chance to understand and even heal generational issues. They help the next generation take the next step, and hopefully learn from our mistakes as well as our growth.

That is the legacy that our stories can become.

# Legacy

Legacy isn't a word we hear very often in daily conversation or give as much attention as we should. Many people assume that legacies are only for the uber-successful or famous—that you have to reach some kind of pinnacle to have anything of worth to pass on. But I don't think that's true. I think we all leave a legacy behind, and our stories can absolutely be part of that legacy.

Legacy is defined in the Merriam-Webster dictionary as "a gift by will especially of money or other personal property: bequest. Something transmitted by or received from an ancestor or predecessor or from the past." If we take the second part of this definition and apply it to our lives, we are constantly reaping the good—and bad—repercussions of the growth, learning, and actions of all those who have come before us.

If you want to see examples of such legacies, ask yourself, what have you learned from your family, from teachers, from people you admire? How have you let that change or influence the way you live your life each and every day? I'm sure we all could list dozens of celebrities who have used their fame and influence to make a difference, but those are not the people we learn the most from. What we need are the stories and experiences from the "average person"—you, me, the people we encounter every day. We all need to know that we can get through the difficult times, and we learn that from the people around us. They are the everyday heroes who inspire us to think differently, to try something new, to keep going even when it seems impossible to do so.

My heroes are people who have let me walk beside them, share in their tragedy and struggles, and see how they keep from letting the difficulties crush their spirits or change who they are. One such hero is my grandfather. Even though he's no longer living and breathing, he will always be my ultimate example of a person to look up to, emulate, and strive to be like. He was an otherwise average man who overcame incredible tragedy and didn't let it make him a negative or bitter person—he remained a kind, generous, loving man until the last of his almost ninety-seven years.

My grandfather lost both his children at different times. No parent should ever outlive a child, let alone all his children, and yet he did. His son, Peter, was killed in a car accident just short of his eighteenth birthday. Peter was a young man with tons of talent and potential—a great student and athlete who was planning to attend Stanford University on a scholarship after graduating from high school. He was well-liked and respected, and the community was saddened by his loss. The outpouring of support received by my grandparents after his death was a testament to who they were and how they raised him.

Then his daughter, Susan, perished at the age of thirty-one in a house fire that also took the life of her husband, Wayne. They left two little girls behind—my sister and I—and my grandparents took us in until a more permanent loving home could be found.

A second such terrible loss could make anyone bitter and angry, but not my grandfather. He and my grandmother poured their love into my sister and me—and into our adopted family. They continued to be incredibly giving people.

I remember asking him once whether all the good that happened in his life was worth all the terrible, difficult things that came with it. He emphatically replied that the good far outweighed the bad—there was no question about it.

After his death, we were overwhelmed with the stories and comments about his quiet generosity: the schooling he arranged for a co-worker so that he could move up in the company, the surreptitious gifts he gave out at Christmas to people who had shown him kindness over the year, the donations of gifts to clubs and organizations, and his incredible legacy of giving to various charities. He was—and continues to be—remembered as a gentleman who had a kind word for anyone who crossed his path, and who was always looking for opportunities to help others. And part of his legacy is that he passed these traits on to all his children and grandchildren.

This legacy has been particularly evident in my brother, who suffered his own trying times when his wife had a devastating stroke at the age of thirty-eight that put her into a rare condition known as locked-in syndrome. He could have been angry and bitter at the cruel circumstances, having essentially become a single father to two young boys and caring for a wife with a serious health condition. But he chose to not let the anger and despair rule his life. Instead, he chose to look for the good—to focus on the boys and take comfort from their achievements as well as his own. The legacy my grandfather left him was the determination and ability to persevere through difficulty and tragedy without letting it stir up anger and bitterness.

For me, my grandfather's legacy is the kindness and generosity he showed and the loving and gentle spirit that touched everyone he came in contact with. I admired him for that, and I strive to be that way as well.

Gramps didn't share his story publicly—in fact, he was so private that we rarely heard him discuss any details. He rarely shared emotion or even referred to the difficult times and tragedy in his life. He was the epitome of "keeping a stiff upper lip." But while we couldn't learn from his own personal story, we had the opportunity to learn from his example, from how he lived his life, and from those who shared with us how he impacted them. In fact, my brother wouldn't even have had this example to follow and learn from had his family not adopted me, my sister, and, by extension, our grandparents.

Through our stories, we have an opportunity to play an active part in deciding the legacy we will leave. Sure, we might pass on financial and material legacies—investments, property, money, personal items. However, the more meaningful legacies are the lessons that come from how we live our lives.

We all have a story to tell. We shouldn't discount ourselves because we haven't won awards or reached some pinnacle of celebrity or obtained a platform from which to proclaim our message to the world. All we have to do is discover the gifts in our own stories and then share them with someone else. And with just that one small (or not-so-small) action, we can change the world.

Our stories of perseverance, of overcoming, of encouragement, of success, and yes, even failure *can* be passed on to someone else. Because we have made it through, because we have learned something new about ourselves, because we have found something (or many things) to be grateful for, we can inspire someone else to do the same. The way you live your life and whether you choose to share your story can each be a determining factor in the choices others make in their lives—possibly encouraging people to take a different step than they might have otherwise.

And that, in my opinion, is a true legacy.

# Something Worth Leaving Behind

A s you think about the legacy you want to leave behind, ask your-self these questions: If you left this earth tomorrow, how would you be remembered? What would people say about you? Your family, your friends, your co-workers? What about your competitors or "enemies"? Would they remember what you did? What awards you won? Your list of accomplishments? Or, will they remember what you said?

And even more important, how would you *want* them to remember you?

My dad first entered my life as Uncle Bruce, with my parents being some of his closest friends. Uncle Bruce was my godfather, so when my parents died in the house fire, there was no doubt in his (or his wife's) mind that my sister and I should be part of their family. I don't know many people who would take in a friend's children and raise them as their own—that alone speaks to the kind of man he was. And though he was my second father, he is the only Dad I remember.

Dad was diagnosed with inoperable stage four lung cancer in the fall of 2014, and he was told that he likely only had three to six months left. Thankfully, we got lucky, and he responded well to radiation and chemotherapy. Three months went by, and then another three. And while he had started walking with a cane and lost a significant amount of weight, his energy was still pretty good.

By summer, though, he started getting weaker. My three siblings and I all lived within a few miles of him, and we all took on a piece of his care and made an effort to spend more time with him. Many afternoons or evenings would find two or more of us (along with his grandchildren and sometimes his friends) sitting with him on his patio and reminiscing about family summer vacations, people we knew, and even some of the things he regretted not taking the time for when he was in full health, like more travel.

As his health continued to decline, we arranged for live-in care—not because we couldn't take care of him, but because we were advised to focus on being with him rather than caring for him. It takes a lot to be a caregiver, and we were already facing the emotional strain of the upcoming loss.

Throughout the summer and fall, his condition slowly declined. He moved to using a wheelchair once his legs could no longer hold him for more than a few steps. His appetite reduced—he couldn't eat more than a few bites at a time, and nothing seemed appetizing to him. Then he was unable to make any movement without help—not even getting himself a cup of coffee. I think what frustrated him most was that loss of independence.

And then, in early December, 2015, he went into hospice care a week before he passed.

What is most important to focus on here is how he handled this news and the limited time that he knew he had left. He was never angry or bitter about his diagnosis—at least not outwardly, not that any of us saw. Instead, he handled it with the utmost grace and with mostly good spirits. He made the most of the days he had, spending time with the people he loved and continuing to make memories. His golf buddies dropped by once a week to catch up on all the news.

His brother and sister-in-law made the drive to visit at least once a month, and he and his brother finally discovered that they were more alike than they ever imagined. Some other friends made the three-hour drive to our city to visit with him after a few years of phone calls and Christmas cards. And as I mentioned already, at least one of his children—sometimes all of us—were usually around as well. He mended a few broken relationships, watched his grandchildren's sports and activities as much as he was able, and made sure to say the things he wanted to while he still could.

We learned a lot before and after his death. We learned that we wanted to face our own difficult times with the same courage and grace and determination he had shown. We learned about the tenacity it had taken for him to bring my sister and I into their family. And we learned just how integral he was in keeping us all connected in the midst of our busy lives.

When we lose those who are important to us, we are never prepared. No matter how much warning we had, there are still words we would have liked to say, hugs we would have liked to share, and yes, stories we would have liked to hear.

We have the opportunity now to capture those important stories, those important lessons and learnings from our own lives. Because when we do, we leave something that lasts.

So, let's go back to those questions I asked.

If you left this earth tomorrow, how would you be remembered? What would people say about you? Would they remember what you did? What awards you won? Your list of accomplishments? What you said?

Maya Angelou said it best: "People may not remember exactly

what you did, or what you said, but they will always remember how you made them feel." Were you generous with your time and your stories? Did you share your struggles and transformations to help inspire and motivate them to do the same? What can you start doing today to live a life that creates a lasting legacy of inspiration, motivation, encouragement, transformation, even healing? You have a gift to share—to one person, or to many. That's love.

All the stories in these last pages are some of the pieces of the legacy left to me, my siblings, our cousins, and anyone who had the opportunity to interact with any of our parents or grandparents over the years. The most meaningful things that I have held on to are how each one of them lived their lives: their kindness, their generosity, their love of life, their love of family. And these are the things I want to embody in my own interactions with others.

I've also been left with more legacies from the many people who have touched my life over the years. The teacher who helped me understand Shakespeare in a modern context. The friend who made the most of her too-short life by embracing adventure. The people I surround myself with on a daily basis who encourage me to be my best. The reader of this book, the listener of my podcast, the follower of my social media accounts.

Yes, that means you as well.

You have contributed in some way to who I am, because every day I'm striving to help you recognize that you have an important story to share. I want to show you that what you've been through—good and bad—matters and can impact someone else.

That is your legacy to me.

Our legacies come from how we invest in others. Because when we focus on investment, on taking the time to really see someone else, that's when we can truly make a difference. It is only by sharing ourselves—our love, our lessons, our time, our stories—that we truly invest in others. When we share the gift in our stories, we create a legacy that can be passed on from one person to the next, creating healing for generations to come.

And that is truly something worth leaving behind.

# Afterword

By Dr. Briar Schulz

*"Storytellers, by the very act of telling, communicate a
radical learning that changes lives and the world:
telling stories is a universally accessible means
through which people make meaning."*
—*Chris Cavanaugh*

I have had the unique privilege of walking alongside of my good
friend Kelly Snider for the past twenty-five years. I have observed
many of her personal hardships and the indelible resilience she has
developed as a result. Kelly embodies the very essence of writing
your own narrative as she continues to craft what she wants her personal story to be, despite some of the incredible challenges life has
thrown at her. I am most inspired by her deep passion to assist others
in healing through personal story writing, and it is an honor to write
this afterword as she shares a path for people to do this work.

As a registered clinical counsellor and post-secondary educator
teaching other counsellors-in-training, I experience the wonder of
storytelling in my daily work.

As an educator, I have the challenging task of imparting rather
dry theoretical frameworks to post-secondary students. A *very* small
handful of students will readily digest this material, incorporating it
into their existing knowledge with little difficulty. The majority, however, will need additional assistance or what I will argue as "creative

data"—also known as a good story—that helps this bland material truly germinate in their minds. Stories provide that sticky factor that enables us to really build on prior learning and understanding. Hearing abstract facts or statistics tends not to permeate our memory the same way that a story does. Stories are in fact the building blocks (mental maps, cognitive schemas) that we use to learn. Essentially, we need stories to fill in the gaps and make us remember.

However, it isn't just any story that makes this information stick. As you are aware, there are good stories, and then there are sub-par stories. The biggest distinguishing factor of a really good story is the connection between data and emotion. As human beings, we rarely learn by gathering facts or bland neutral information. We need the emotional content to assist us in continuing to build the cognitive structures or schemas that already exist. In other words, the emotional content of a good story helps us connect with what we already know and becomes the true glue in ensuring we remember the story. Furthermore, the deeper we emotionally connect with a story, the stronger the memory.

Now in terms of what is happening in the brain during this time (now that we have fancy brain scanners to see this stuff while people are still alive), there are these two sections dedicated to language reception called Broca's area and Wernicke's area. These regions in the brain light up like Christmas trees when someone is taking in a really good story, and that activity doesn't happen to the same degree if someone is just hearing facts or statistics. But this isn't the best part. We now have scientific research showing that when someone connects emotionally with a story, they release this wonder chemical called oxytocin, also known as the love hormone. You remember back when you were madly in love with someone, and you felt so ridiculously giddy? Oxytocin was responsible for that feeling. But this hormone is also known as the moral wonder as it helps produce compassion, goodness, moral thinking, trustworthiness, generosity, all that's truly good in people. In fact—probably my most favorite fact of all, because I teach this to students everyday—oxytocin is responsible for empathy. So, to develop more empathy in others, we need more stories to create more oxytocin to create more empathy! As you can see, stories are the most powerful, important tool in existence, and they can be life-changing for all of us.

Could there possibly be a downside to any of this? Well, just one word of caution here (and this is me with my psychology hat on): stories are also what gives us this term the "availability heuristic," one of those dry terms you might have been introduced to in an introductory psychology course. The availability heuristic is where we rely on our "stories" or our knowledge about something without possibly understanding the facts. One of the best and saddest examples of this was after 9/11, where anyone wearing a turban was immediately and universally judged. The heinous terrorism on September 11, 2001, led by one extremist group, left many people judging other people from a wide variety of cultures and religions based on assumptions made from their own availability heuristics.

It is essential to remember that stories don't always behold facts but rather interpretive experiences. Furthermore, we have a powerful ability to project our subjective interpretation onto our stories, which can cloud factual data. However, this knowledge doesn't need to detract from the ability of a story to transform another; it is just an essential component to remember when listening to any story.

In my work as a clinical counsellor, the knowledge that stories aren't necessarily factually accurate can actually be a very helpful tool for understanding the power of both deconstructing and reconstructing a narrative. In other words, narrative theory in counselling utilizes the power of story by helping a client understand what narratives have contributed to who they think they are. In the same essence, narrative therapy assists a person in understanding they have the capability to create new narratives, and that past narratives don't have to define them. In addition, when working with people in conflict, you can assist people in taking the time to listen to and empathize with the other person's story. It doesn't have to be their story, and they don't even have to like it, but they do need to be able to respect it and then work towards possibly creating a new story together (if appropriate). Narrative therapy has profoundly changed my work in counselling as I witness people harness the power of story and their ability to control the narratives they tell themselves.

Narrative therapy has been found to be particularly effective in working with trauma. To be clear, this isn't about trying to erase a traumatic memory by merely "rewriting a narrative" or deconstructing it to somehow diminish or downplay the impacts of the event. Such a simplistic approach would be both naïve and counterproductive. Rather, the benefits of narrative therapy extend far beyond a singular trauma narrative to consider the highly complex, contextual layers that contribute to the effects of trauma. Examining such issues over time through ongoing levels of narrative therapy and advanced storytelling offers a traumatized individual an opportunity to gain agency where they have previously felt completely disempowered and dysregulated. As we all continue to live in this complex world filled with assumptions that are constantly being shattered, understanding how to live beyond trauma has become a necessity. I would argue that learning to craft our own narratives with authenticity and courage offers much hope in beginning this process.

In this book, Kelly introduces how and why you should begin your own storytelling process. She cleverly embeds key aspects of her own personal story to enhance your engagement and learning. As mentioned before, I can personally attest that her story has been shaped and redefined to allow Kelly the control in her personal healing and recovery from significant trauma. I encourage you to sit back, find a cozy space, and enjoy the storied parts of her book while also beginning your own journey of learning the impact of telling your story.

*Briar Schulz PhD (RN, RCC) is a registered nurse and registered clinical counsellor. She holds a BSN from the University of British Columbia, as well as an MA in Counselling Psychology and an interdisciplinary PhD from the University of Victoria. In addition to maintaining a private practice in Langley, she has over twenty years of experience teaching at the undergraduate and graduate level. Dr Schulz is also passionate about community engagement and is a trainer for the Crisis and Trauma Resource Institute of Canada.*

# Gratitude

There aren't words enough to describe how thankful I am for all who have helped me make this book possible. The truth is that every day, there have been people and situations that have encouraged me to keep moving forward. It's been more than fifteen years since I first felt there was a book I needed to write, and I know that it's almost impossible to remember every person who helped get me here. But I will do my best to cover those who have left an indelible mark on my journey.

First, to my family, those who have come before and those with me still today: You all have an invaluable role in my story, and I wouldn't have it any other way. You've taught me, you've challenged me, you've shaped me, and you've encouraged me with your strength, courage, grit, and determination to pursue wellness, excellence, and joy.

To Deb, Jana, and April: You listened every time I tried to make sense of my experiences, challenges, and lessons. We have shared meals, getaways, long walks, laughter, and so many of the difficult conversations and moments in our lives.

To Lisa L, who was there at Canyon Ranch when I first realized the power and strength that my story had to encourage and inspire others: Our conversations and visits, sporadic as they may be, helped me to keep moving forward with this goal.

To Alison, Barbie, and Briar, the early readers of my messy, unfocused, and sometimes pain-filled writing: Thank you for your encouragement and your honesty.

To the coaches and mentors who have helped guide me along the way (Jon, Kim, Brielle, Emily, and more): You have encouraged me to dig deeper, to acknowledge my fears, and to do it anyway.

To all the co-authors in The Gift in Your Story: thank you for trusting me through the process and for being vulnerable with me, with our group, and with all our readers. The lessons you taught me helped make this book finally happen.

And to so many more good friend and teachers: This list would be exhaustive, and I would be sure to leave more than one of you out. Just know how incredibly appreciative I am for your friendship, support, encouragement, and care.

Finally, to you, my readers: I hope that you are inspired and encouraged to revisit your own stories, find deeper healing, and use them to do the same for others and leave a lasting impact on the world around you.

From the bottom of my heart, thank you.

# About Kelly Snider

Kelly Snider is a bestselling author and story curator who thoughtfully collects and preserves stories through creating events, writing books, interviewing guests on her podcast, and facilitating life-changing story workshops. She is an expert at extracting stories and identifying value and strength within the narrative. As an acclaimed event producer, she highlights her clients' individual stories, needs, and goals. Since the 1990s, Kelly's story-focused events have raised over twelve million dollars net for charities around the world.

Kelly brings her mission of supporting and inspiring others to life through sharing the stories that connect us all, and her generosity in sharing her stories of overcoming has emboldened thousands to find the freedom and the strength to share their own. Through her platforms The Power of Story Conference 2017, the Epic Exchanges Podcast, and the Epic Exchanges collaborative anthologies, she helps people to find the true gifts within their stories and share them in order to inspire others and transform lives. She thrives in finding ways to connect people, whether that is through attending charitable events, sharing food and wine, or simply having an engaged conversation. She also may be slightly obsessed with hummingbirds, the ocean and deep and meaningful connections.

To connect with Kelly, please visit her website:
www.KellySniderAuthor.com
or check out her podcast Epic Exchanges